Expand Your Psychic Skills

EXPAND YOUR PSYCHIC SKILLS

ENID HOFFMAN

Whitford Press

1469 Morstein Road
West Chester, Pennsylvania 19380 USA

Expand Your Psychic Skills
by Enid Hoffman

International Standard Book Number: 0-914918-72-9

Typeset in 10 pt. Paladium on Compugraphic MCS/8400
Edited by Julie Lockhart and Anne Driscoll
Cover design by Bob Boeberitz
Typeset by Camilla Ayers and Kristen Orlando

Published by Whitford Press
A division of Schiffer Publishing, Ltd.

This book may be purchased from the publisher.
Please include $2.00 postage.
Try your bookstore first.
Please send for free catalog to:
Whitford Press
c/o Schiffer Publishing, Ltd.
1469 Morstein Road
West Chester, Pennsylvania 19380

Manufactured in the United States of America

First printing, May 1987

To Frank David Molinski, my son, my publisher, my employer and above all, my friend.

"Life is never dull...when the road is open before one."
—*Lawrence J. Bendit*

Contents

Introduction

Most of us have been led to believe that human beings are limited and fragile creatures, capable of perceiving only a small portion of the world in which we live, and almost powerless to affect it in any real way. We have been taught that we are helpless victims, that we must make our way through life almost blindly, accepting the conditions that befall us as the will of God, fate or coincidence. We are told that this earthly existence is all there is and that we only go around once. With such a dismal and pessimistic perspective, is it any wonder that we war with each other, pollute our planet and grow sick in body and spirit?

Well, I don't buy it. I don't agree that we humans are ignorant, weak and ineffectual. Nor do I accept that our lives are determined by the whim of some omnipotent being whose reasons are beyond our comprehension.

I believe we are all gods, sparks of Divine Mind, capable of creating our own realities and taking charge of our lives—this one and those that will follow, in this world and in others. I believe we have potential as yet undreamed of by most of us. I believe we can expand our awarenesses, extend sensory perceptions, heighten mental skills, increase physical aptitudes and intensify emotional experiences, just by choosing to do so. In so doing, we'll discover that each and every one of us is *psychic.* Being psychic is simply a matter of using our natural skills in a more complete, integrated and expanded way.

This book is based on the premise that, like me, you believe there is more to life than resigned, plodding acceptance, and you have chosen to develop your power, to become all that you can be. Actually, this book is about choice. As you read it, you are choosing to expand your potential, your so-called psychic skills. As you use the following techniques, you are choosing to expand your psychic skills into your everyday life.

Life is a series of choices, and every day in everything you do you are choosing your reality. Whatever you experience reflects the choices you have made and at any time you are free to change any of your decisions. When you realize this and become aware that you are continually exercising free choice, that you are responsible for choosing—or not choosing—you empower yourself. Now you can be and do anything you choose; the decision is yours entirely. Life becomes exciting!

The material contained herein is meant to be shared. Most of the techniques have been shared by many people already. Through sharing, you benefit both from using the techniques and from being exposed to the experiences of others using them. You move into a state of cooperation with others who desire the same things you do, who are seeking to develop and expand their psychic skills and their understandings of themselves, other people, nature and the invisible realms. As a result, of your cooperative efforts, you can begin to eliminate competitiveness, antagonism, fear, hostility and violence from your world and live in harmony with all other beings. You'll discover that we are all part of the same consciousness. We are all in this together.

As you continue on the path of exploration, never lose your sense of adventure, your desire to learn and grow with each new discovery. Use the material in this book to enrich yourself and your relationships. As you get in touch with your deepest feelings, your most honest and sincere thoughts, you'll find yourself rewarded through expanded knowledge and abilities. Above all, keep your pursuit of self-knowledge joyful. It is easy and fun—if you believe it is.

1

Psychic Fundamentals

We have many mental skills which we use continually—to create, grow and function in the world. All of us think, perceive, analyze, intuit and cognize. The more uncommon mental skills are usually called *psychic skills*, but they are only an enlargement or extension of "normal" mental skills.

We are all psychic. Each of us has the potential to expand our everyday mental processes into greater, farther-reaching, extra-ordinary "psychic" skills, and thus to gain expanded happiness, wisdom and meaning in our lives.

The Mental Trinity

If you were to look at the inner workings of a watch, you would probably see several wheels moving separately within, held in rhythm by the pulses of the main flywheel. Together these separate wheels work efficiently to keep the time mechanism accurate. In some ways this is how the mind works, for at any one time there are many different mental processes working simultaneously within us. There are at least three different minds or "selves" which operate independently yet in conjunction with each other. Each has a separate but equally important part to play in our functioning.

I define these three minds, or selves, as the *conscious self*, the inner or *natural self* and the *higher self*. It is not important what we call them so long as we recognize them as distinct and separate, each playing an important role in the whole person.

The Conscious Self

The conscious self or conscious mind is the part we commonly think of as "I am." Also known as the human or social self, it is the part that thinks and speaks. It communicates by talking. It uses reason and logic, evaluates and makes choices. Its choices give direction to the subconscious or natural self. The conscious self accepts or rejects incoming information and tells the natural self what to integrate into your character, personality and belief system. The conscious self is the director, the decision-maker, the goal-setter.

The conscious mind is masculine. That is, its force is penetrating, directing, commanding. Its role is that of leader, teacher, parent, designer. It is the initiator, the beginner of all things. The quality of the material used in creation is directly related to the work of the conscious self.

The Natural Self

The inner or natural self is directed by the conscious self. Although the natural self has the power and urge to grow, that growth occurs within the framework *designed* by the conscious self. Psychotherapists call this part of the mind the subconscious. I prefer to think of it as my inner, natural self.

The natural self never sleeps. It is always aware of the exterior world, scanning it for anything that will be of interest to the conscious self. The conscious self always retains the power to decide whether to act and how. This constant awareness of the outer world—even when the conscious self is sleeping or unconscious—means that the natural self can be influenced by things other than its own conscious self. For example, doctors and nurses in operating rooms must be careful what they say about a patient, for the literal meaning of their speech is absorbed and integrated into the patient's subconscious mind even when unheard by the conscious self. Patients' conditions have been known to plummet after a careless doctor commented, "I don't think this one is going to make it."

The subconscious mind, or natural self, is feminine. Its job is to manifest the intentions of the conscious self, to create the patterns and designs of the conscious self and to achieve the goals of the conscious self. The natural self has no will of its own but accepts the direction of the conscious self. This impressionable part can be taught and trained to fulfill the desires and wishes of its own conscious self—or any other self. Advertising, for instance, can direct the inner self. As a result, we sometimes find ourselves desiring, purchasing or eating things we never intended to, impulsively reacting to an advertiser's suggestion.

The natural self is an excellent term for this part of us for it is a unit in the world of nature, participating in the life flow with all other natural units. It has power to commune with other aspects of the natural world and feels unity with them. This is why many people are sensitive to weather changes. All our physical body systems, both voluntary and involuntary functions, are controlled by the natural self and it possesses *body wisdom*, or the knowledge of how to maintain and develop the body to maturity.

It was once believed that the conscious mind could have no control over involuntary behavior. However, the science of biofeedback has proved clinically that when the desires of the conscious self are understood by the natural self, the subconscious self will usually cooperate. Body functions such as respiration, temperature, heart rate and blood flow can be changed by the subconscious self under the direction of the conscious self. Biofeedback subjects can learn to alter their body temperatures by as much as 20 degrees.

We can increase our knowledge of the inner self by observing body functions and movements. "Body language" is a form of communication the inner self uses to express its feelings, thoughts and attitudes (often in contrast to the verbal expression of the conscious self).

Body language experiment: Try some different body positions to feel how your body expresses inner states and conditions. Change your posture. Slump and hold that position as you tune into the feelings and thoughts it evokes. Now stand up straight and feel the difference. Thrust out your jaw so that it precedes your body as you move. Now thrust your whole head forward as you walk and sense what this communicates. Sit and cross your knees. Then open your legs wide. How do you feel about these positions? Which way are you most comfortable and why? Clench your fists tightly as you experience what that means. Now let your hands hang loose and open. Next, cross your arms tightly across your chest and keep them there long enough to interpret what this gesture means.

Exercises for building self-confidence: You can work with body behavior to retrain your inner self to new attitudes and a new self-image. Decide on a change of body behavior that will communicate a specific message. Through repetition and reminders that this is the body expression you want to manifest, this behavior not only will become habitual but actually will be integrated into your subconscious framework. For example, a self-confident body stands tall and erect, reaching upward with the head. The face smiles, the arms and hands are relaxed. Stand and walk around the room in this manner to demonstrate to your inner self the body behavior that illustrates self-confidence. Direct your inner self to change both its attitudes and body behavior. Show it exactly what you want and lovingly insist it is capable of accomplishing this.

Handwriting exercise to increase confidence: Your handwriting is also body language and it expresses your inner states and conditions. Have your handwriting analyzed and then work from the outside in, changing your writing style to create a corresponding inner change. For example, look at where you cross your t's. The lower the crossbar is drawn on the stem, the less confidence is indicated. Start deliberately crossing your t's higher but not above the stem. The stem represents your current capabilities, and you can reach for the top if you build your self-confidence.

As we tune into our bodies, we are tuning into our own natural selves. The acts I perform are those I choose, but the *way* they are performed is an expression of the state of my inner self. The inner self is always trying to communicate with its conscious self, striving continually for union and connectedness. When the conscious self is embarrassed, for instance, the inner self may respond by producing a blush or stutter. Overwhelmed by stress, I may get a cold, develop ulcers or even cancer.

One of the marvelous aspects of the inner self is its attunement to the natural rhythms and seasons. Its knowledge of the cyclic nature of our Universe and its ability to work in cycles are fantastic. This sensitivity to cycles assures you of waking in the morning and going to sleep at night. This inner clock can be set to wake you at a specific time if you convey your wish efficiently to your subconscious self and no inner barrier exists to conflict with that wish.

Waking up exercise: Decide what time you actually want to get out of bed. Then think of how you would like to accomplish this in a *ritual* that begins when you are still asleep and concludes when you are fully awake. A ritual is a series of steps used to accomplish a purpose. The inner self is ritualistic and any ritual, repeated often enough, becomes a habit.

Now you are going to create in your imagination a ritual whose purpose is to have you awake and ready to go at a specific clock time. (Interestingly, the subconscious self *always* knows what time it is without seeing a clock.) Sit down and relax physically. Impressions are always more effective on your subconscious when both your mind and body are relaxed. Close your eyes and imagine your physical body lying sound asleep in the bed. In that picture, see a clock with the time you want your body to begin waking up clearly visible. See your body become restless and start to move. Your eyes open slowly. Bring the clock into the picture again, its time coinciding with the opening of your eyes. Let your eyes focus on the imaginary clock as it reflects the time you have chosen. Now visualize your body sitting up, then easily rising from the bed. Imagine your eyes focusing on the clock face for the final time, fulfilling the purpose of the ritual, as you see the time you want to be fully awake.

Your inner self is literal and does not understand ambiguity so whenever you direct it to manifest your desires, give it absolutely literal instructions. Once you have imagined this waking ritual, affirm your intention that your inner self will do as you wish. Your natural self is quite fond of accomplishing the tasks you give it. It loves to display its skills and perform for you and others, and can do nearly anything (within the realm of possibility and probability) that you can conceive.

Physical survival is a joint effort of the conscious or human self and the natural self. While the human self is busy balancing the checkbook or planning a dinner party, the natural self is aware of everything going on in the environment, watching for anything which might threaten your survival. If and when a threat appears, the natural self alerts the human self to it, attracting its attention so that action can be taken. The natural self has a much greater range of observation than most of us suspect and, if encouraged, it can alert us to threats far away in space and time. Developing that potential is one of the objectives of this book.

Here is an example of this "joint effort" at work. Recently my sister and I were on a long trip. I was driving and listening intently to her conversation when suddenly my attention was drawn to the car speedometer. I was going too fast and immediately slowed the car, realizing that my natural self had attracted my attention as a warning. Sure enough, within minutes we passed a patrol car parked by the side of the road. In this instance, the danger was not of having an accident but of getting a speeding ticket.

You can increase the span of your subconscious background perception and enable your natural self to communicate with you quickly and effectively if you desire. Begin now to observe closely the way your attention works. Notice what attracts or distracts it, and ask yourself *why*. As you come to understand the process you will be able to use it more efficiently.

The Higher Self

The higher self is also known as the deep unconscious or superconscious mind. This part of the mind goes beyond the world of nature and encompasses all that is. It is our connection with the divine nature or essence. It has been called a guardian angel and the universal mind. This part of you can take on many forms in your mind to portray its multi-sided nature. It can be encountered in fantasy, imagination and dreams. It holds the key to your destiny as well as the reasons you chose to incarnate. Contained within its subtle memory body are the memories and accumulated wisdom of previous lives. These remain outside your awareness until the conscious self is ready to integrate such knowledge into its functioning.

The higher self is concerned with the evolution of individual consciousness as well as the evolution of humankind. Its world view is broad, without bias or prejudice. The higher self is never blinded or deafened by acculturation and works to help the other selves recognize truth and falsity. Its fully integrated feminine and masculine sides work together in complete harmony. On a higher level, this self reflects the potential of the other two selves.

The other two—conscious and subconscious—so often at odds with each other, can obtain much help from the higher self when their objectives are those the higher self considers worthy. There are conditions that block communication and help from the higher self, however, and we will uncover some of these as we proceed.

The human self is centered in the head, the natural self is centered in the solar plexus, and the higher self is centered in the subtle body just above the physical head. Knowing the approximate location of these centers makes it easier to communicate with them. When communicating with the inner self you can focus your attention on the solar plexus, near your navel. When praying or sending messages to your higher self, you can target the area above your head. This helps ensure that your attention-energy flows to the right channel.

Communicating with Your Selves

In order to expand your psychic abilities, you need to develop good, clear communication between your human, natural and higher selves. I find this is easiest when you are physically and mentally relaxed. If you are not already skilled at meditation or other relaxation techniques, you may want to try the following exercise to establish a calm, serene state, sometimes called an *alpha* state. In this light trance, your human or conscious self grows still and quiet, and your inner or natural self is free to send you messages in the form of impressions, feelings or pictures. Your everyday cares and concerns are placed "on hold" temporarily and you feel a sense of inner peace and contentment.

Relaxation technique: Sit in a comfortable chair and loosen any tight, restrictive clothing. Begin breathing slowly, easily, deeply. Inhale, hold your breath for a moment or two, then exhale with a sigh. Repeat this breathing pattern again and again, using a slow, even rhythm that seems natural for you. Now begin to relax your physical body, starting with your toes. Wiggle them a little, then let them go limp. Move your focus up to your feet, then your ankles. Feel them loosen and release any tension therein. Direct them to relax. Now focus your attention on your calves; feel them relax and grow limp.

As you release the tension in your extremities, you'll begin to experience a sensation of warmth slowly rising from the bottom of your feet into your body. Let this sensation increase until you feel yourself glowing, tingling with a gentle, soothing warmth. Continue to let your attention move up your body as you direct yourself to relax gradually, little by little, muscle by muscle, until you are completely calm, quiet, serene.

Take your time and really enjoy the sense of total relaxation enveloping and permeating your body. As you become more practiced, you'll find you can achieve this light trance state much more quickly and retain it longer. Whenever you're ready to return to your usual, waking state, simply start again with your toes. Wiggle them, then move your feet, stretch your legs, and slowly open your eyes. You'll feel rested and rejuvenated.

Another technique I use frequently in my workshops and for my own purposes is something I call a fantasy game. This technique allows your inner self to communicate information to your conscious self, in a way that many people have found easy, natural and productive. During a fantasy game, you experience a shift from normal wakefulness to a state of reverie where the contents of your unconscious are freed and float to the surface. The process involves a series of steps: physical relaxation (you may use the above relaxation technique or another you prefer), quieting the activity of the ego or linguistic self, and becoming a passive observer to what your inner self is presenting.

A fantasy game is engaged in for the purpose of learning something about your life, history, feelings, problems, beliefs, etc., and the purpose is usually determined before you begin the game.

Also called a guided fantasy, a fantasy game requires a guide to direct the flow of consciousness as it comes into the participant's awareness. This guide can be either another person or a taped voice reading a fantasy game "script."

Here is a fantasy game script. This game is designed to help you recognize yourself as you exist in your inner and outer worlds, and to improve communication between these different aspects of yourself. You can tape record it or have a friend read it to you.

Fantasy game "Your natural self—past, present and future": Sit in a comfortable chair and begin breathing slowly, deeply, rhythmically. Close your eyes and relax. Imagine you are walking down a road or path and see another figure approaching you. This being is your physical or natural self. As this being comes closer to you, begin to notice the different parts of its body. Are there any that you dislike or find offensive? Focus on these parts and pay attention to any feelings that arise in you. How are your attitudes toward your body preventing you from attaining what you want? Now see your natural self clothed in its favorite outfit. You'll notice that it chooses to wear what it finds most comfortable.

Look behind the figure of your natural self and you'll see that there is another figure walking down the path, approaching both of you. This figure is you as a child, displaying prominently some physical feature that you had strong feelings about at that age. Pay attention to any feelings you had then as well as those that still exist now in relation to that part of your physical body. Have your feelings changed with time, or are you still being influenced by old, out-dated attitudes?

As you observe the image of your past self, recall all the things you liked about yourself then . . . and those you didn't like so much. Take a few moments to examine the attitudes you once held about yourself. Now begin a dialogue with your past self. Inquire what this self always wanted and never got. In your fantasy world, you can give your past self whatever it wants; proceed to do so. Now talk to this self reassuringly, forgiving it past transgressions and healing past hurts.

When you two have completed your conversation, bid farewell to the image of your past self and see it return to the forest.

Now watch as a third figure begins walking toward you down the road. This is the physical you of the future, the body you expect to have in years to come. What does it look like? Are you satisfied with it? Are there parts of it that you don't like or want to change? What other feelings are associated with this being?

At this point, you may wish to stop and write down your feelings, impressions and insights about you as a natural, physical being. You can return to this meditative state afterwards and continue with the next stage of this fantasy game.

When you are again relaxed and ready to resume your visualization, return in your imagination to the same road you stood on before. Your present-day natural self is still there waiting for you, but the past and future images are gone. Now you will see another being coming toward you down the path. This is your vision of your social or human self as it exists in the human world, the part of you that interacts with others in a conscious way. Notice what it is wearing; it has chosen its outfit to create an impression for others in the social world.

What is your reaction to this part of yourself? As your social self stands beside your natural self, pay attention to the similarities and differences between the two. They may look like identical twins, but chances are they appear quite different. How do they move? Is one more graceful, at home in its body? Is one bigger than the other? Does one of them try harder to attract your attention? Are you more satisfied with one of them than the other?

As you watch, the two images of you move apart and a third being appears between them. It glows with a noumenous light, and is clothed in colors and fabrics that integrate your two worlds: the social/human and the natural. This figure represents the best of both worlds, a "composite you" that displays your own unique and special potential.

Hold on to this image as long as you can, and pay attention to the feelings that arise with the image of your ideal self. Ask your deeper mind to describe ways for you to achieve this perfect image and to integrate the two parts of yourself. Allow the scene to evolve if it seems to want to do so. When you feel you have gone as far as you can, gradually come out of your meditation and write down your experiences, thoughts and feelings.

Using the Pendulum

We all can become *dowsers*. A dowser is someone who is able to draw information from deep inside through the use of specific techniques. Most dowsers seek information about the outside world, such as locating water beneath the earth, but we can use the same techniques to get information about our inner worlds. By using a pendulum and teaching the inner self "pendulum language," we can get answers to our questions. When we teach our conscious and inner selves how to use the pendulum we also are showing our desire to be in close communication. That wish often develops into a phenomenon we all have experienced on rare occasions: *knowing* the answer as soon as we have phrased the question. But we must begin by taking each step in turn, training our selves in this new language skill until they can work successfully with it.

It is easy to make a pendulum; all you need is an object approximately the weight of a fifty-cent piece suspended on a string or chain. You can use a pendant, a key or a heavy button.

Hold the string or chain end of the pendulum between the index finger and thumb of your dominant hand (the one you write with) and swing it back and forth in front of you. You may keep your elbow on a table if this is comfortable for you. Whatever position is most comfortable is the one you should use. As you swing the pendulum back and forth, tell yourself (aloud or silently) that this motion means "yes." Then, stop the pendulum's motion with your other hand. Let it dangle quietly as you ask your inner self to swing it the way you did. Keep encouraging your inner self to do this, for it can do it easily if it is so inclined. Take turns demonstrating consciously, then asking you inner self to do it as you watch.

As soon as you feel the slightest motion, compliment yourself on learning this new skill and move to the next word, "no." This is a sideways swing—from left to right and back again. Demonstrate this to your natural self as you repeat its meaning. Again, ask to be shown how well it can imitate you. Continue these steps, teaching your inner self a diagonal swing for "maybe," a circular swing clockwise for "good" and a counterclockwise circling for "bad." These circling motions can be used for "like and dislike," "comfortable and uncomfortable," as well as other polarities about which you may want information.

Once you have taught your inner self these motions, you need to teach it to stop each one on command. Here is where we must recognize one aspect of the natural self. *It interprets everything literally and does not comprehend ambiguity.* This is very important to remember in all your dealings with your inner self. If you should ask your self "Will you stop swinging the pendulum?" it will probably keep swinging "yes" to indicate its willingness. This is the correct answer—literally. To get your inner self to actually stop, just quietly and authoritatively say "stop."

It is amazing to see the control you can develop in pendulum use. Your inner self learns very quickly. You now have a means whereby your conscious and inner selves can have a dialogue and get to know each other much better. Since your inner self holds all memories and you are dependent on it for recall, you now have a new method for regaining this information.

Having a dialogue with your own selves also involves an exchange of energy. There will be a flow of energy between the two which is invigorating and satisfying. As you focus love on your inner self, it will intensify its devotion to you and your interests. Develop courtesy and consideration in all your contacts with it. Drop all denigratory remarks you used to make about yourself and replace them with compliments. Whenever you hear your speech include self-insults, stop and retract, apologizing to your natural self, and very quickly you will find you automatically cease any negative programming. Awareness of negativity is the key to losing it!

Here are a few rules to successful internal dialogues. Never ask your inner self stupid or frivolous questions. They are as insulting to your inner self as they would be to a friend. Do not ask questions to which it does not know the answer or it will lie to satisfy you. Do not hold a preferred answer in your consciousness or that is the answer you will get rather than the truth. Your natural self is used to reflecting your thoughts and desires. Keep an open mind while questioning and convince your inner self to answer truthfully. Do not ask questions about the future unless your inner self has been trained in precognition or prophesy. The purpose of using the pendulum for dialogue is to get information about your beliefs, values, self-image and emotional states. You also can investigate body conditions and their causes. Start a notebook to record the information received from these conversations.

Pendulum exercise for finding lost objects: You can ask your inner self to find a lost object. Close your eyes and relax. Without specifying where, visualize yourself picking up the object and looking at it. Affirm "now it is found." (It is never truly lost to your inner self.) Your inner self will share its knowledge with you and soon you will remember or see in your mind's eye where the "lost" object is. If this doesn't happen, you can use the simple yes-

and-no code with a pendulum and begin a series of questions designed to determine the location of the lost item. Start with a large area and keep narrowing the area until you can pinpoint the object's place. Go there and pick it up!

Problem Solving

We have two ways of solving problems. One uses conscious mental abilities to arrive at solutions, the other involves our inner selves and utilizes their assistance. Following are the steps for using the second method.

1. Create an intention to solve a particular problem and define the problem as clearly as possible.

2. Gather as much information relating to the problem as possible. Write down both the problem and information relating to it.

3. Give all of this to your natural self to work on. Affirm that your inner self can and will come up with a solution.

4. Give the problem time to incubate and be integrated with all other relevant factors within you.

5. Expect to receive insight into the problem and ideas for possible solutions at the appropriate time. You will.

6. Check the suggested solution to see if it is the best in your opinion.

Note: If you ask your inner self for help before going to sleep, often it will provide some excellent ideas by morning.

Let's investigate your ideas about problems. Get out your notebook and print the word PROBLEM at the top of the page. List all your associations with that word and your attitudes about it. How negative is your view toward problems? Are problems bad or good to have? Would you like a problem-free life? Would you like to change your concept of what a problem is? Can you conceive of a problem as a challenge or an opportunity? Can you become wiser by encountering and working with problems?

Now head a page with PROBLEM SOLVING and list all the ways you can deal with a problem. Ignore it. Go around it. Sweep it under the rug. Jump over it. Find someone to help you get through it. Do you feel good about working on problems or does this depress you? List some of the methods by which you have solved problems in the past. Can you perceive of problem solving as an enjoyable activity? If not, why not?

It is by solving problems that we grow and learn. Problems arise because of ignorance; they are all opportunities for gaining wisdom. Problems show us where we need to develop better skills or obtain more information. Realizing that problems are beneficial can help us in our search for well-being and happiness.

Exercise for developing better concentration: Through suggestion and repetition you can train your natural self to let you concentrate without interruption whenever you desire to do so. Tell your self that if it detects anything threatening, *really* threatening, to your welfare it may draw your attention to that, but not to anything else until a specified time. Tell your self what time you want to be alerted to change your activity. Then begin concentrating, confident your inner self will guard you and alert you at the correct time.

Most of us have fearful and uncertain inner selves who constantly draw our attention to one thing after another and keep us from concentrating on our objectives. Many of our inner selves have been allowed to become so "talkative" we that have little peace.

You can change this habit by spending "quality" time listening to your natural self and recording thoughts that arise into your awareness in return for silence when you need to work "alone." Chatter grows excessive when we don't listen; the cure is an improved listening style. We can begin by noticing exactly what our natural selves want us to be aware of and thus learn much about their needs and beliefs. In your notebook, start lists of the things your inner self wants you to perceive and have a dialogue with it about them.

We all are born curious and once we learn to speak we start to ask questions. As children we may have annoyed others with incessant questioning. But as we got older, our questioning subsided and by the time we were adults our curiosity had faded until it was nearly non-existent.

In order to change our lives for the better and to achieve growth and increased happiness we must arouse that innate curiosity which stems from the desire to know. Answers only come to us in response to questions. Discovery is the delightful experience of finding an answer that was present, but undiscovered. We begin to realize, through discovery, that multitudes of answers lie around us everywhere, just waiting for the proper questions. There are many questions that have no answers, but every answer has a question. The task is to match the questions with answers. To do that we must create and recreate our questions over and over until we find their mates.

Exercise for getting answers to your questions: Get out your notebook now and play with some questions. Write out each question in various ways such as:

Why does he or she criticize me?

Why do I react to criticism by becoming upset?

Why do I choose to be upset by criticism?

Ponder each question by sitting back, eyes closed, holding the question in your awareness for a moment. Let the question dissolve and observe your inner response to it—pictures, images, ideas or memories. If you like, you can ask your inner self to give you associated beliefs, values or ideas that also lie in your mind. Through continuing questions we can obtain many answers that will be helpful in the re-creation of a more integrated personality.

We human beings are marvelously designed, created with all we need to accomplish the purpose of incarnation on planet Earth in a single lifetime. That purpose is to evolve from ignorance to wisdom through a series of small steps, developing a deeper understanding of reality with every step. Each time a bit of ignorance dies a small portion of wisdom is born—to remain eternally ours.

2

Life Energies

All creation depends on the interaction of two forces: male and female. This universal principle exists everywhere, in everything. Even the act of procreation itself requires the energy of both the male and the female. According to some creation myths, in the beginning all was one. Nothing happened. The All was dormant. The first act of Divine Mind was the division of itself into two parts so that through their relationship creation could begin.

Hermetic philosophy calls this the principle of gender. In it, masculine and feminine are considered two halves of one whole. Known as *yang* and *yin* in the East, they are uniquely different and opposite in nature, and neither can exist without the other. Their interaction creates what we know as life.

We have symbols to help us understand the nature of these two life energies. Fire symbolizes masculine or yang energy, the radiant energy that moves outward from a central point of spirit. It may be likened to the sun, and its radiance is penetrating and stimulating. In contrast, water symbolizes feminine or yin energy. In different cultures it is called *mana, prana, chi* or *ki* and many other names. This female life energy flows like water and is affected by the moon. Associated with the subconscious and unconscious minds, it is sometimes called *psychic energy*.

Our physical bodies reflect the duality of life energies. The brain has two hemispheres which control opposites sides of the body. The left side of the body, dominated by the right brain hemisphere, is the center of feminine intuition. Our psychic abilities reside here. The right side of the body, dominated by the left brain hemisphere, is the seat of masculine intellect. We use this side in our day-to-day, rational functioning. The nervous system also is divided into two parts, one for controlling each side of the body.

In most people, either the fire or the water principle is dominant. Fire type individuals are usually outgoing and active. They are the leaders, the initiators and the organizers. Persons ruled by the water principle are sensitive and tend to be introverted. They enjoy solitude and mental rather than physical activity. These two energies are often referred to as positive (masculine) and negative (feminine).

The *caduceus* is another appropriate symbol for the movement of the two energies through the body. Most of us would recognize the caduceus, which depicts two snakes entwined around a winged staff, as the symbol of the medical profession. But it has an older, "occult" (or hidden) meaning as well. The *Dictionary of Mysticism*[1] calls it the wand of Hermes, which originally was a triple-headed serpent, now two serpents—one black and one white—representing the struggle between good and evil. The *Dictionary of All Scriptures and Myths*[2] describes the caduceus as the symbol of aspiration through the higher mind, the two serpents signifying wisdom and desire.

In some yogic disciplines and Eastern religions, the serpents represent the *kundalini* force or serpent power as it moves through the body, coiling upward along the seven energy centers or *chakras*. (For more information about the chakras, see chapter 7.) According to kundalini yoga, the caduceus is not an arbitrary symbol, but an actual depiction of the path this energy takes as it travels from the base of the spine to the crown of the head.

This kundalini energy contains the potential for higher consciousness and exists within each of us. In most of us, however, this serpent power lies dormant at the base of the spine, waiting to be awakened. Quite likely, the serpent who showed Eve the fruit of the Tree of Knowledge in the Biblical story of the Garden of Eden symbolizes this kundalini power.

Color exercise for balancing energies: When we project life energy outward, we can choose to add thoughts and feelings to that energy. Energy flows, imbued with our intentions. Thus, if you feel you have too much of one energy, you can counteract the condition through visualization. For example, if you feel tense or frantic, you can compensate for an excess of masculine energy in your body by visualizing yourself surrounded by a silvery blue cloud. If too much negative or feminine energy is making you too withdrawn and subdued, envision yourself surrounded by golden, pink or rosy-red light. If you want a surcharge of both energies together, see them as a field of colors swirling around you. Breathe the colors into your body, knowing that your body's wisdom will absorb exactly the amount it needs of each. Now see the colors blend together, growing lighter and lighter until they become a brilliant, clear light whirling around you.

Color exercise for transmuting energies: Emotions and feelings accompany flowing, moving life energy. In its essence, this energy has no color; it is pure light. But often this energy is accompanied by feelings that we associate with specific colors. You can learn to transmute the quality of a feeling from one that is unpleasant to one that is preferable merely by changing its color. (For more information on colors and their uses, see chapter 4.)

I taught this exercise to one woman who found that it was especially helpful during arguments with her husband. "The technique kept me so busy that I didn't react the same way I had before," she told me. "My different response changed the pattern of our relating."

When someone is directing angry, resentful, depressive, or other unwanted feelings toward you, begin by tuning into what he or she is experiencing. Draw that feeling toward yourself and imagine the color that best represents the quality of that feeling. If the person is angry, perhaps the color red is appropriate. If s/he is depressed, you may see a dark grayish-blue or black.

Allow this energy to flow into your space, inhale it and visualize it moving down to your solar plexus where you will transmute it. Quickly swirl this energy around in your torso, and visualize it changing color. If you want to calm angry red energy, you might choose to transmute it with a visualization of blue. Pink is associated with love and compassion, and can help change another person's hostile or resentful emotions into ones that are more loving and pleasant. It's also useful when you're feeling insecure, unloved or uncertain. Yellow or gold might be chosen for courage, steadying and strengthening. As you exhale, direct this color-tinted breath at the other person. Keep breathing in this manner for a minute or two, or until you feel the work is complete. This exercise is helpful for another reason, too. It helps you to open yourself up to another's experience—an important part of developing your psychic skills.

Breathing exercise: This exercise helps you to draw in psychic energy. It can be performed from at least once a day to as often as three or four times a day if needed.

Sit comfortably in a chair with your back erect and your head up. Cross your feet at the ankles and clasp your hands in your lap. Take a deep breath to a rhythmic count of eight, then hold that breath in your lungs for a count of twelve. Now exhale through your nose to a count of ten. As you breath out, direct the outflow of air at the roof of your palate so that it makes a slight purring sound as it leaves your nose. Repeat the entire exercise five times. This exercise allows you to gradually accumulate psychic energy. You are creating a "savings account" of this energy, acquiring a bit more each time you perform the exercise.

Pine tree exercise: Feminine energy exists everywhere, although it is stronger in some places and in some objects than in others. Pine trees, for example, contain much of this psychic life force; it flows within them like the sap. Stand near a pine tree and you can feel the cool, refreshing negative ionic power in it. Take a nap beneath its branches, stroke its needles, hug the trunk to tap into the tree's life force. For an everlasting supply of this energy, you might consider planting your own pine tree near your home.

Using Your Feet

Our hands and feet breathe, too—not air, but life energy from within the earth and from the atmosphere. The palms of our hands and the soles of our feet filter that life energy as it is drawn in and discharged through our pores. Our feet take in life energy from the earth and absorb it; our hands pull in the atmospheric forces released from the sun and moon. Our bodies breathe through the pores of our skin, constantly inhaling energy through these tiny vortexes, which are miniature chakras.

When we speak of someone who is fearful, we say that person has "cold feet." This is an accurate description. Fear draws energy away from your hands and feet into the center of your body, and so your appendages grow cold. When you are relaxed, feeling safe and secure, the blood flows outward, filling your hands and feet with warmth and life.

Exercise for your feet: You can help your feet and hands draw in energy by using your imagination. Relax. Close your eyes and visualize energy streaming in and out of your feet in a rhythmic, regular pattern. Envision the energy as colorful and potent—red or gold to envigorate, blue or silver to calm. Look at your feet and send loving, caring attention to them.

If you have a problem focusing on your feet, imagine you are holding a magnifying glass that helps you to see them better. Pay attention to the sensations in your feet and toes—feel your socks, the touch of your shoes, the floor beneath your soles. After you've experienced pure sensation in your feet, repeat the exercise with other parts of your body.

Getting energy from dew: Another energy source available to our feet is dew. On its way to earth, dew absorbs much life energy which can be taken in through the feet so a walk in dew-covered grass can be most refreshing.

You can use dew as a symbol in your visualization exercises. Picture yourself walking across a dew-drenched meadow. Feel the cool, wet dew on the soles of your feet, see yourself stroking blades of dew-covered grass with your hands and rubbing the moisture on your cheeks.

Happy feet: Get comfortable, relax and close your eyes. Begin this technique for circulating life energy throughout your body by focusing on your toes. Imagine them laughing. As you do so, they actually begin to wiggle. Imagine the life energy being drawn in through the soles of your feet as your toes wriggle. Visualize that energy as a color—whatever color seems comfortable to you. This feminine, psychic energy restores good health and energizes your physical body. You also can see any blocked, crystallized energy breaking up and becoming liquid.

The strong pulse of life flows from your toes to your head and as the energy fills your body, you feel envigorated. All seriousness and gravity disappear in its path and the bubbly sensation of laughter travels from your toes, up your legs, through your torso to your head. You feel yourself growing taller as the pressure of gravity is pushed aside by the power of levity. See this fluid energy like the water rising in a fountain. Feel the energy cleaning and purifying all your subtle bodies and energy fields.

Massage

Reflexology is a science which deals with energy patterns in the body. Every organ in the body has an energy connection in the hands and feet. By treating a point in the hand or foot and channeling the correct level of etheric energy flow, a practitioner can treat the corresponding organ or body part.

When pressure on a point in the hand or foot causes sharp pain, it indicates that energy has collected in the corresponding part of the body and crystallized. The reflexologist then attempts to break up the crystallization by massaging the point on the hand or foot. A dull ache that occurs as the point is pressed indicates that not enough energy is reaching the corresponding organ; the reflexologist will massage that point to restore an adequate flow of energy.

Reflexology technique for your feet: You can be your own reflexologist and give yourself a foot massage.

Get a round pencil or rod with a rounded tip, then sit comfortably in a straight, armless chair. Bring one foot up and rest the leg across your thigh. First massage your whole foot, pressing lightly but firmly with your thumbs and fingertips. Now take the pencil and press against the foot between each toe, carefully and slowly. Rock it back and forth as you press. Now take each toe between your fingers and thumb and stretch it out as far as you can. Pull it slowly but firmly out as far as it will go. After stretching it, massage each toe vigorously. Now give that foot an all-over massage before you put it down and start on the other.

Hand massage exercise: This exercise is similar to the above foot massage. Stroke each finger and pull it out firmly until the knuckle cracks a bit. Massage your palm with your opposite thumb. Also massage the area between the thumb and index finger. This spot is connected with the head and massaging it can help relieve headaches.

We tend to use our muscles to bind up feelings we don't want to express. The muscles are a storehouse for energy or *mana*. This energy can solidify and crystallize, becoming immovable. Deep muscle massage, reflexology, *shiatsu* (Japanese finger pressure massage), Rolfing, Reichian and some other forms of muscle therapy seek to break up deposits of repressed thoughts, feelings, emotions that keep the muscles stiff and tense. Even lighter forms of massage such as "Swedish" massage sometimes are accompanied by a release of these pent-up feelings. You can start to become aware of your repressed energies by paying attention to any thoughts and emotions that arise while you're having a massage.

Tapping the Source of Energy

Seven centimeters below your navel is the source of your life energy. It is called the *Hara* and is the center of gravity in your physical body. The Hara is your source of personal power.

When you inhale, your breath moves toward the Hara, but you can aid this process in your breathing exercises by using your imagination. Visualize your breath being drawn deep into your body, into the Hara. Practice this often so that your body will continue the process automatically when you are not focusing your attention there.

You might also want to tap the Hara point with a finger to graphically illustrate to your unconscious mind where and what the Hara is. This reinforces your intention to send energy there.

The Hara has the power to transmute and transform energy. For example, if someone who is angry with you sends you hostile, fire-red energy, your Hara can transform it into blue serenity. If you experience unpleasant emotions such as fear, insecurity or resentment rising from your subconscious mind, you can send them to your Hara and ask that they be transmuted into other, more desirable qualities.

To move energy from the Hara center, all you have to do is create the intention to do so. For example, if you want to walk down a crowded sidewalk and have the crowds separate like the Red Sea, merely project energy from your Hara center outward to open a path before you. To strengthen an arm or leg, you can visualize powerful energy flowing from your Hara center into that limb.

Hara experiment: To demonstrate the power of the Hara, try this experiment with a friend. Face each other from opposite sides of a room. Begin walking toward each other. When you meet, your friend will attempt to push you over. But you have used the power of the Hara to stiffen your body. Imagine power rising from your Hara strengthening your entire torso, making your body as strong as steel. (Your friend, however, should not do this.) When you meet, ask your friend to try to shove you. He or she will find it nearly impossible to push you over. As a basis of comparison, try the experiment again, but this time do not draw on any of your Hara energy. See how easily you are pushed over!

Subtle Energy Fields

Each of us has a personal atmosphere composed of at least three and probably seven energy fields. The fields are also called *subtle bodies*. They interpenetrate each other and exist at different vibrational rates. Some sensitive people can see these subtle bodies surrounding the physical body, like bubbles or halos of light. When someone speaks of seeing a person's *aura*, this is what he or she is seeing.

The finer and more subtle the vibrations, the larger the subtle body and the more space it occupies. These fields are composed of etheric substance of differing grades. Each field has a label to identify its function.

The first field contains the prototype of the physical body and supports and maintains that body. The next is called the emotional field; it is affected and changed by what we feel. The third, called the mental field, is affected and changed by what we think, by our attitudes and views. These three inter-penetrating fields also affect and influence each other, relating in a very personal way. When we get to chapter 7 on healing, we'll see how the health of each body affects the well-being of the others.

Everything in the Universe has a life field. All life fields affect and are affected by all other life fields. These life fields have magnetic power, drawing to themselves what is attractive to them and repelling that which they find antipathetic. Each field has an individual pattern of attraction and repulsion. The life field most easily detected is the electromagnetic field.

Have you ever walked into a meeting in the midst of a heated debate? Or been present at a sporting event during an exciting game? That group of people has generated a "group energy field." Individually, each of us creates the same phenomena. Your inner self is continually reading the atmosphere in your environment—whether you are with a group of friends, in a packed movie house or alone in an empty room. With practice, you can teach your inner self to communicate this kind of information to your conscious mind so you'll be better informed about your environment.

Personal objects such as jewelry and clothing retain the energy vibrations of the people who wear them. This is why psychometrists can read the personality or life of an individual simply by holding a ring or watch that person has worn—and tuning into the energy patterns still clinging to the object.

Houses hold the energies and experience patterns of their residents long after they have moved on. We often take on the coloration of the places in which we live, absorbing emotions and thoughts that have been left behind by others. If you move into a house that has an atmosphere filled with violence and anger, for example, you can be influenced by it and your own energy field may change. Or, you may be calmed by living in a house that has a peaceful, relaxed atmosphere.

Atmospheric house cleaning technique: Any disagreeable atmosphere can be cleansed, sweetened and transmuted. One method is to drop a pinch of salt in the corners of any room which feels unpleasant. If visitors leave some negativity behind, cleanse the space they occupied by sprinking a bit of salt there.

How can you avoid having your energy field adversely affected by others? First of all, you can affirm your intention to repel all harmful thoughts and feelings while being receptive to good ones. You can strengthen your own force field by keeping your thoughts and feelings upbeat and harmless. You tend to attract the same sort of energies that you give off. Thus, if you project angry, resentful, hateful thoughts you'll likely attract harmful energies to you. Conversely, if you send out positive, loving energy, you'll invite the same kind of thoughts and feelings. Imaging and affirmations also can help strengthen your subtle bodies.

The white light of truth technique: This technique is also known as "the white light of protection" and is an ancient practice used throughout the world. The word *white* needs to be understood as clear, colorless light, not the color white as we perceive it in paint. This clear, colorless light has no golden tones (like sunlight) but is pure light itself. By visualizing it, you draw it into your energy field, transmuting and purifying any properties that would attract harm. Surround yourself with it and it will keep you immune from harm.

You can use this technique in many ways to provide many different types of protection. For example, when you are driving or flying, visualize the vehicle you are traveling in completely enveloped by white light to protect you from the possibility of an accident. If you fear you have been exposed to a germ or contagious illness, surrounding yourself with white light will shield you from infection. You can protect loved ones and your pets by imagining them surrounded by white light. By visualizing white light all around your home you can safeguard it against fire, wind or water damage, and intruders.

Protecting yourself from psychic abuse or attack: Psychic attack occurs when a person (or group of persons) directs toxic, harmful, malefic ideas and feelings at someone else. Sometimes this is done unknowingly; that is, the "attacker" doesn't realize his or her energy is hurting another individual. Sometimes, however, this is done with conscious, malevolent intent to induce pain or distress. You can protect yourself against psychic attack or abuse by using a combination of the white light protection visualization and the color transmutation exercise described earlier in this chapter.

Sometimes a person or group decides that someone should suffer or be punished in a way that causes pain or misery. Often this is done out of self-righteousness, and the feeling-energy that is transmitted is malefic. Many people accept the idea that they deserve to suffer, however, I don't believe this is true. The following exercise can help relieve this type of distress, whether it is the result of others' psychic attacks or your own guilt.

Begin by relaxing and breathing deeply, drawing the harmful or threatening energy toward you. Picture the associated color of that energy: red relates to anger, black to guilt, "poison" green to jealousy or resentment, dark gray-blue to depression, etc. Then you can change it in your solar plexus into either loving bright pink, or into a color that corresponds to another positive emotion. Light, clear blue can tranquilize and "cool" anger, golden-yellow stabilizes and balances agitated nerves, purple heals psychological or spiritual disturbances, and rosy-red uplifts depressed emotions. Make sure the colors you use are transparent, glowing, pure and beautiful. Finish by surrounding yourself with the clear white light of protection to shield yourself from future attacks.

Ions

Not only are our personal atmospheres affected by other people, we also are influenced by *ions* in the earth's atmosphere. Ions are miniscule units of electrical energy spinning through the environment. The atmosphere is composed of positive, negative and neutral ions, and their balance—or imbalance—impacts our moods.

When the atmosphere is highly-charged with positive ions, as it is just before a thunderstorm, the air is heavy, humid and oppressive. It causes an unpleasant sensation of pressure in the body and a desire for relief. Positive ions are also generated by the movement of hot, dry air. This condition occurs naturally in the deserts of the Middle East and Northern Africa, stimulating people into behavior they normally inhibit and control. These winds have been known to influence individuals' moods so severely that violence and criminal acts increase during certain times of the year when the wind activity is high. An excess of positive ions also can be created by hot air blowing through the heating systems in our homes and offices. People who are particularly sensitive to ionic imbalances can counteract an overabundance of positive ions with a device called an ion generator.

Negative ions are given off by plants and falling water. They are cool and refreshing. This is why we feel both tranquil and invigorated when standing near a waterfall or in a pine forest—we are literally revitalized by an electrical charge. This is also why many people experience mood changes and a sense of relief after a thunderstorm.

When the ion ratio is in balance, we feel better, function better and are better able to heal ourselves or resist illness. Our social relationships are enhanced and we can think and act clearly. You can use your pendulum to dowse the ionic condition in your home or workplace. If you discover too many of one type of ion, the following exercises can help restore balance in your own system.

Ion balancing exercises: An abundance of positive ions can be corrected by sitting in a comfortable, yet erect position with your feet squarely on the floor and slightly separated. Place your hands in your lap, also separated. Relax and inhale slowly, deeply. Hold the breath to a count of seven then release it easily. Imagine tiny, blue-white sparks of cool, refreshing energy whirling counterclockwise around you. Now begin to inhale these sparks, breathing deeply, slowly and easily. Continue to inhale, hold the breath to a count of seven, and exhale in a rhythmic pattern. Perform this breathing exercise seven times.

If your atmosphere contains too many negative ions, you can correct it by sitting erect and comfortable as described above, but with your feet touching. Touch the fingertips of your hands together (but not the palms) and hold your hands at chest level. Exhale slowly and when your lungs are empty count to five. Next, breathe naturally for five breaths while you visualize vortices of warm energy spinning around you in a clockwise direction. Inhale these sparks with a deep breath, then exhale again and count to five. Repeat this exercise five times. At the end of either breathing technique, change your position immediately and put the entire process out of your mind.

Energy is the stuff from which all things derive existance. It is intelligently conscious and can never be destroyed. Our own energy fields and those around us in our environment can be directed by conscious choice and formed through the use of our psychic skills. As we become aware of these many layers of consciousness, we begin to understand life itself and our own lives take on an aura of excitement and vitality.

Notes

1. *Dictionary of Mysticism*, edited by Frank Gaynor (New York: Citadel Press, 1968), p. 31.

2. G. A. Gaskell, *Dictionary of All Scriptures and Myths* (New York: The Julian Press, 1960), p. 135.

3

Levels of Being

One winter I was driving in the mountains of Vermont, when suddenly my awareness expanded spontaneously. As my perception altered, the landscape seemed totally new to me and I became aware of a dimension of consciousness I had never known before. The landscape came alive dramatically to me, pulsing with life and vibrancy. Every mountain, every tree, every rock and blade of grass transmitted its delight in life. I was amazed to see that even the asphalt road and the metal of my car teemed with this life force and I laughed aloud in exhilaration.

In those few seconds I had glimpsed the consciousness that exists within all things. The experience faded as quickly as it arrived and I have never had it again. But I remember it vividly and the knowledge I gained from it has never been lost.

Consciousness

Consciousness is everywhere. It is the state of being of the Universe. We live in a sea of consciousness that is the mind of our planet. The earth is an entity with its own mind and consciousness. The consciousness of the Universe is like a book with many chapters; each chapter is an entity with its own identity. Together the chapters combine to make a greater entity.

Once you understand that consciousness and life are one and the same, existing everywhere, in everything, you come to realize that the terms "animate" and "inanimate" are meaningless. All matter vibrates with life and consciousness. Life and consciousness, like waves of light or energy, are in constant motion. This vibrating motion swings in a measured beat. It is this rhythmic beat that gives us a sense of time passing.

Think of the pulse of consciousness as a strobe light, flashing on and off. Let's say that ten flashes per second is our usual sense of one unit of time. If, however, the light only flashes five times instead of ten, we will experience only half as much and time will feel as if it is passing faster. Now, if we change the rate of speed again and the light blinks twenty times in a second instead of ten, we will experience twenty flashes of awareness in the same unit of time. We see more, experience more, and time seems to have slowed.

For example, many people experience a sudden apparent slowing of time when danger threatens. Events roll by as if they were on slow-motion film. This gives them plenty of time to cope with what is happening and to make appropriate choices. This increased perceptual ability results from a change in consciousness which allows a higher ability to act. In normal waking consciousness, for instance, brainwaves beat at a certain rate. When you meditate and are in an *alpha* state of consciousness, the beat of your brainwaves decreases and you experience a change of consciousness.

Consciousness forms the background of our experience. It is wholistic and feminine in nature. Though we know it's there, it is not what our attention is focused on at the moment. Instead, it forms the context in which the central subject matter exists. You could liken consciousness to the background of a painting or the orchestra playing behind a piano solo. Consciousness gives us our spatial sense, our knowledge of where we are in relation to other beings in space.

Consciousness exists on many levels and we will begin to explore these in this chapter. The records of all our experiences and memories are held in our consciousness. Consciousness contains not only our individual, current-life memories but also the wisdom of the ages, records of our past lives and our future potentials.

Each of us has a *personal consciousness*, filled with all our personal memories, thoughts and experiences. We also have *group consciousness* for each group of which we are members: human, racial, national, family, etc.

The records and memories of all events experienced at every level of consciousness are always available to you. As you become agile in moving to other levels you'll find that you can recall past experiences on these different levels.

Recall is best if you shift to the level on which the event or events originally occurred. For example, if you have had experiences in meditation that you want to explore further, you must return to the meditative state to recall them again vividly. All past dreams are available to you, too, and often recur when the "dream work" is incomplete. There are many levels of consciousness available to the "dreamer." As you explore them you will find that you can move to various dream states where the learning you desire can occur.

Animal, Plant and Mineral Consciousness

The inner self is called the natural self because it is in tune with the whole of nature—the tides, trees, streams, planets, animals, birds, minerals. And because the natural self is attuned to all things in the natural world, it is capable of communicating with them. The natural world also includes the *elementals* or nature spirits—fairies, elves and devas—who inhabit it. Although most of us have never seen these elemental spirits, literature abounds with references to them.

We can change our present attitude of hostility and fear, which results in the destruction of the environment, into one of loving cooperation with the natural world—to our mutual benefit. If we are to survive on this planet, we must change this relationship and come to consider ourselves equals rather than superiors, co-creaters not exploiters.

Communication with other life forms is possible for each of us. Author and metaphysician Rudolf Steiner even suggests that this is an important part of achieving enlightenment. In his book, *Knowledge of the Higher Worlds and Its Attainment*, he recommends that persons seeking enlightenment conduct exercises with a stone, a plant and an animal. Such persons must be open first to the possibility of intelligence in these life forms, then quietly, without judgment, observe them with respect and appreciation. Thoughts and feelings are passed from human to stone, plant and animal in turn. In time, if the seeker remains open and receptive, s/he will be able to sense a feeling communication emanating from the stone, the plant and the animal—each in a distinctly different manner that is characteristic to its level of consciousness.[1]

Animal Consciousness

Animals are sensitive to our thoughts and feelings. Horses are said to be able to "sense" fear in a rider and there are many accounts of cats and dogs who have journeyed hundreds of miles to find the people they cared about. It isn't necessary for us to communicate with our animal friends verbally, all we have to do is mentally transmit thoughts or emotions to them.

One evening I decided to try an experiment with my son's cat, a big, black, long-haired feline named Sam. As Sam lay curled up comfortably on the sofa I imagined a yellow tiger cat sitting beside him and devoted my attention to that imaginary cat. Suddenly Sam sat up and glared at me, swishing his tail angrily, then jumped off the sofa and left the room.

In his books *Kinship with All Life* and *The Language of Silence*,[2] author J. Allen Boone tells of his experiences in the art of communication with animals. By developing a pattern of humility, sincerity and patience he was able to communicate with dogs, birds, snakes, insects and many other non-human forms of life. Once he dispensed with his superior attitude of being an "educated human" he was able to establish friendships with monkeys and other animals.

Boone believes the key to communicating with animal consciousness is three-fold. First, we must respect our animal friends as our equals and stop thinking of ourselves as educated, more intelligent, superior beings. Second, we must become "like little children," curious to learn what the animal is trying to tell us and eager to listen. Third, we must stop using our rational, thinking minds and trust our intuition. This involves communicating with our hearts and what he calls the "inner spaces" rather than with words.

Plant Consciousness

Plants are sensitive to our feelings and will thrive when caring attention is paid to them. In the 1960s, lie-detector examiner Cleve Backster discovered that his ordinary house plants could read his mind. By hooking them up to a polygraph machine, he could even measure their responses to his emotions and thoughts. He also found that distance was irrelevant; plants could maintain a link with a person over spans of many hundreds of miles. Backster's experiments are covered in detail in *The Secret Life of Plants*, by Peter Tompkins and Christopher Bird.[3]

At Findhorn in Scotland, a community which attempts to live in harmony with all of nature, nature spirits were contacted by members of the community and found to be highly intelligent. Findhorn members were able to recreate the relationship between humans and the plant world by remaining receptive to the wisdom transmitted by the elementals in the devic kingdom. The knowledge passed on by the elementals was used by the people of Findhorn in the care of their gardens. As a result, what had been a barren, sandy wasteland was transformed into an oasis of trees, flowers and vegetables. The alliance between plants and humans benefitted both groups. You can read more about Findhorn in books by David Spangler and other residents of this remarkable community.

Plants have been used for thousands of years to remedy ills in the human physical body. More recently, Bach Flower Remedies, which contain the essence of plants rather than their physical substance, have become recognized for their ability to heal the human spirit. Conditions such as timidity, depression, sorrow and anxiety can be aided by one or a combination of Bach's flower essences. One remedy, called the Rescue Remedy, helps people deal with traumas such as the loss of a loved one.

Through telepathic communication with the plant world, we can develop harmonious relationships with the plants entrusted to our "keeping." Improved communication and understanding between species will lead to a better quality of life for all earth's creatures, for all consciousnesses are integrally linked and dependent upon each other for survival.

Mineral Consciousness

Mineral "life" is unobservable to most human eyes, however, minerals have consciousness, too. It is the "breathing" action (expansion and contraction) in crystals, for instance, that makes them useful as transmitters in radios and TVs and provides the "tick-tock" rhythm of our watches. Variations in mineral consciousness manifest as differences in hardness and color. The minerals in our physical bodies are very much connected to those in our earth, and we can locate gemstones to enhance our health, well-being and individual consciousnesses. This is the original purpose behind wearing birthstones.

Crystals are the most evolved form of mineral consciousness. Quartz crystals are a combination of silicon (or sand) and water, formed by pressure, temperature and energy. Most quartz crystals come from Arkansas, Brazil and Madagaskar. Quartz' ability to store energy makes it useful as computer chips; its focusing properties are utilized in lasers. But quartz and other mineral crystals also can be used for healing, meditation, protection, to increase psychic powers, to balance emotional energies, for dowsing, and in countless other ways. My editor "plants" small crystals in her garden to help her vegetable plants grow bigger and stronger.

Heat and pressure can transform crystals. For example, nature's application of heat and pressure can change amethyst (purple rock crystal) to golden-yellow topaz or citrine. People have even baked crystals in bread to alter color and consciousness!

Choosing a crystal: Crystals are much more popular and available now than they were even five years ago. They are sold in gem stores, metaphysical shops and even some gift shops. (Lead crystal, such as that used in making glassware, is different.) *Double terminated* crystals are pointed at both ends, *single terminated* ones have only one point. Energy is directed through the points, so if you are going to wear your crystal, it's preferable to choose one that is double terminated.

Let yourself be drawn to a crystal. When you find one you feel an affinity for, pick it up, hold it in your hand and ask "for me?" You'll receive the appropriate impression. *Don't* have a hole bored through a crystal—this is equivalent to giving it a lobotomy! *Don't* round off its points—you can kill the crystal! (Note: Crystal balls have specific purposes and uses.) You can never "own" a crystal, you can only be its guardian.

Clear quartz crystals can be used for almost any purpose. Rose quartz crystals are especially good for healing emotional problems and for calming anxiety or fear. Amethyst crystals may be used for meditation and to balance energies as in polarity healing. Garnets increase imagination, rubies enhance intuition.

Caring for your crystals: You should clean your crystal to flush away any negative or unwanted energy. There are many ways to do this, but some of the most common are placing it in sea water for twenty-four hours, holding it under warm running water, setting it in sunlight or moonlight for twenty-four hours, burying it in earth for forty-eight hours, or burying it in sea salt for two to seven days. You will want to clean your crystal from time to time to rid it of any negative energy that it might have picked up from the environment. If you are using it for healing purposes, cleanse it after each healing session. Clean your crystal if another person handles it. If you have a particularly stressful or frightening experience while wearing or carrying a crystal, clean it as soon as possible to wash away the energy of that experience.

Store your crystal in a small bag made of natural fibres: cotton, silk, linen, wool, leather. Treat it with respect and love, as you would a friend entrusted to your keeping. Remember, a crystal is a living entity!

Charging a crystal: Choose a date when the sun or moon is in your astrological sun sign. The best time is the new moon when both the sun and moon are in your "sign." Perform this exercise between noon and midnight.

Make sure you have cleaned your crystal beforehand. Create an altar for your crystal and place it there on a piece of silk or linen. Living flowers, burning incense and three lighted candles should accompany the crystal on the altar.

With your dominant hand (the one you write with) describe a circle in the air around the altar. Now lay your hands on the altar palms down, dominant hand on top of the other hand, and affirm—or chant, or sing— what powers or qualities you wish to increase in your crystal. Repeat this three times, then close your affirmation with a chant "aaauuummm." To open the protective circle, redraw it with your hand. Leave the candles to burn out and remove the crystal. Place the crystal in a small box to protect it when not in use. If the crystal is intended for another person, give him or her the crystal *in* the box.

Mineral consciousness meditation: The best space for this meditation is an attic or upper floor, far away from the ground and street noises. You may do this meditation with a single gem or several. Amethyst, tourmaline and turquoise, as well as quartz crystal, are good stones to use in meditation. Make sure the gem(s) has been cleaned before you begin, then place it on a piece of dark cotton velvet. Do not use artificial lighting during this session, but you may light a few candles if you wish. Let your eyes dwell on the gem as your mind becomes quiet and receptive to the radiations of the stone. Allow its vibrations to unite with your own. Let its intelligence communicate with your consciousness.

When you feel ready, shift again into normal consciousness by stretching and focusing your eyes on some other nearby object. Shrug your shoulders to loosen them. You may wish to make notes of the experience in your journal.

Every particle in the Universe breathes, contracting and expanding in its own particular rhythm. For every bit of mineral consciousness "out there" we have a resonating one "in here" that recognizes its "kin." They radiate their nature which is perceptible to the highly-developed mineral consciousness within our own bodies. Thus we can seek out and find in the earth those minerals we need to aid us in our personal growth.

Consciousness sensing experiment: Do this experiment with a friend. You are going to try to sense the different types of consciousness that exist in different natural things. Use a plant, a crystal or gemstone, an ordinary stone from a garden or driveway, a cup of sea water, a shell, a stick of wood and something synthetic, such as a new plastic comb or a ballpoint pen (one that hasn't been used and thus has few human vibrations attached to it). After letting your inner self examine each object briefly, close your eyes and ask your friend to remove one item. Use your consciousness-sensing ability to determine which object is missing from the group. Take turns sensing and keep track of your scores. I find children often are quite good at this!

Awareness

Often the words "consciousness" and "awareness" are used interchangeably. However, these two states are distinctly different. Consciousness is the pulsing vibration that is the essence of all things. Awareness is the individuating "I AM" in each of us. Wherever I am, my awareness is also. When I move, my awareness goes with me. When I focus my awareness on something, I perceive that thing. Through my physical sensory organs I am aware of sights, sounds, tastes, smells and touch. Through higher sensory perception I am aware of much more.

We experience awareness and consciousness simultaneously, in much the same way as we perceive both foreground and background together. Awareness is particular, whereas consciousness is wholistic. We are *aware* of what is in the foreground at the same time we are *conscious* the background. For example, as your awareness focuses on a sailboat on the lake, your consciousness is surveying the entire landscape.

Awareness is an aspect of masculine power. It is linear, sequential and related to time, to our experience of past, present and future. It has the capacity to focus on and work with one thing at a time. As we expand our awareness to perceive more of consciousness, we strengthen our skills for accomplishing our goals. As we expand our skills, our awareness will let us move into any field or level of consciousness we desire at any moment in time or space.

It is in awareness that we make the choices which become impressed on our inner selves. Those choices become "intentions" and prevail until superseded by new choices. Awareness stimulates and directs consciousness, which then works to make our intentions manifest in the physical world. Through developing our awareness, we can penetrate deeper into the many levels of consciousness, using our awareness and consciousness together to create the existence we want.

I find I can communicate new concepts best by using symbols. To understand the difference between awareness and consciousness and how they work together, we can use the pyramid as a symbol. Perhaps in so doing, we also can uncover one of the fundamental meanings of the pyramid.

If you look at the back of a $1 bill you'll see a good depiction of this symbol. The bottom portion of the pyramid represents consciousness, existing as a material form. The apex, which is another, smaller pyramid itself, rests on the flat top of the larger pyramid and represents awareness. Think of the pyramid as being composed of layers or striations, starting with the broad band at the base which symbolizes universal consciousness. It is here that all memory, all events and all human creations are contained. The layers become successively smaller as we move toward the top of the pyramid, until we reach the apex which is pure, radiant, focused energy.

Pyramid meditation: Close your eyes and bring to mind the image of the pyramid. The peak is made of shimmering light, the light of your awareness. Now see this glowing light move downward until it fills the layer just below it, the top layer of the material pyramid. Continue letting the light of your awareness spread layer by layer into the mass of consciousness until the entire pyramid shines with a radiant glow. This visualization shows awareness expanding and penetrating consciousness. As your awareness grows to incorporate more of the pyramid, you become more capable of understanding and utilizing the wisdom contained in your own consciousness and in the universal consciousness.

Observation technique: This exercise frees ideas and allows them to arise into your awareness. You first will need to cease all inner "chatter" temporarily. Sit quietly, relax physically and mentally. Ask your inner self to pull thoughts in from the left side of your body and mind, then move them across to the right side where they will exit. Follow these thoughts as they pass through you, respectfully recognizing each one. Gradually, they will slow down and you should continue to observe them until you feel they have completed. Now rest quietly as you invite all aspects of your being to participate in this exercise.

Ask to receive enlightenment within a specific category. You may inquire about your current beliefs, attitudes or convictions. You may want to know about events in the past where part of you became stuck and stopped growing. All of your past experiences, good and bad, reside in your memory. They exist below awareness where they influence your reality and often limit your potential.

This process allows some part of your internal experience to separate from the inchoate mass so you can observe it. It arises into awareness as a thought, an idea, a symbol, a picture or a memory. As it separates, it becomes available to you for understanding.

All of us have had moments in the past when we were unable to resolve some experience. That experience, as yet incomplete, needs resolution before we can grow. All those past, incomplete experiences needed something which was not available to us at that time. In your altered state of inner observation, create an "intention to know" and the willingness to learn about that incomplete past experience.

You may want to begin with your birth and silently request any incompleted experiences from that time to come into awareness now. Again, wait patiently. If nothing arises, move into the second year. When some memory, symbol or idea arises, remain an impartial observer. Refrain from analyzing or thinking about it. Allow it to happen without interference, comment or judgment, without making assumptions or jumping to conclusions. Look for details and create the intention to recall them later.

It is best to conclude after one or two recollections so that you can transcribe your experiences in your notebook. As you write down what you became aware of, you may feel inclined to develop the theme further. To get the greatest benefit, realize that this particular event has significance for your inner self and ask that you become aware of that significance.

Fantasy game "The house": Consciousness pervades space, existing in levels or layers which correspond to rates of vibration. These levels are also called *planes of consciousness*. Awareness travels through space and through many planes of consciousness, and we have the potential to expand our awareness to include many more states and levels.

Imagine consciousness as occupying space horizontally, like many floors in a building. Awareness moves up or down like an elevator, stopping at one floor or another so you can explore consciousness on that particular level.

You can think of a building as a symbol for the different levels of personal consciousness. Each floor of the building represents one level of consciousness; various rooms on each floor may be seen as containing experiences and memories. By moving into a trance or meditative state and asking your inner self to use the building as a symbol, you can explore your character, personality and programs.

At a workshop I was giving, a man taking part in this fantasy game saw two buildings. One was a ramshackle hut in a dump, the other was a partially completed new house. He found one of his college teachers and his father in the basement constructing the new house. In the discussion following this fantasy, he said he was very comfortable in the shack at the dump, but felt strange and uneasy in the house his father and teacher were building for him. The new house was neither designed nor built by him, but by others. This experience helped him understand his current career dilemma.

In your fantasy game, use a house with two floors, a basement and an attic. The basement will represent the past, and the parts of the past you are preserving. Here the unconscious or subconscious can be explored. The first floor will represent your everyday, conscious experiences. The second floor will stand for your dream life and the unmanifest side of your personality. In the attic you will encounter future plans and expectations, as well as some of the higher planes of consciousness that filter down into the present.

Close your eyes, relax, breathe deeply and get comfortable. Use a simple countdown from ten to one to complete the process of moving into a light trance state. Now, silently request the symbol of a house in your imagination which you will view from the outside. In your mind, circle around it, looking at all the outer features of this house. Observe the front and the back of the house, noting any specific differences. You will remember all details for later analysis so just enjoy observing and continue the fantasy.

Choose either the back or front door to move fluidly into the house's first floor. Here the first room encountered will hold objects that represent your everyday concerns. Note them without analysis, then move to a door which leads into the basement. Go downstairs and begin your exploration of the foundation of your being. Realize that you are looking at symbols from your past, symbols of what is stored in memory, waiting to be dealt with at some other time. Be a good observer, but do not become involved with anything in particular.

After a suitable time, go up the stairs again and continue up to the second floor. Here your dream world deposits its symbols, and your higher will holds its goals. Here feeling expresses itself in colors and objects that denote some of your many current relationships. If there is a particular relationship you want to explore, find a room with that sign on the door. Enter and look for clues that will provide insight into that relationship. There are as many rooms as you have relationships. Take your time on this floor, observing without judgment and memorizing for future work.

When you feel ready, move up to the attic, the top floor where your hopes for the future lie around in symbolic form. You'll see objects that relate to stories of your past planning, your goals yet to be achieved, talents yet to be demonstrated. Here you may find symbols of wisdom which you can explore as well as secrets of your destiny or fate. There is much treasure here—look for it. Again, there are rooms with signs on their doors.

Whatever you wish to find is here and you can explore those rooms simply by deciding to go through their doors.

When you are satisfied with your visit to the attic, go back downstairs to the first floor where again you will find many rooms. Here your present circumstances can be seen from new angles, different viewpoints. You will find a door with a label for each current role you are playing. Inside each room is a stage set which allows you to see how your role is being played and how you might improve your role-playing. Roam this first floor, investigating every room you wish.

When you have explored this house to your satisfaction, move out through one of the doors and go back to the front of the house. Observe the façade. This symbolizes the way you believe you are seen by other people. This façade represents your persona. Again observe it without criticism, noting every detail for later analysis. When you have finished, slowly come back to waking consciousness by first wiggling your toes, then stretching your legs. Stretch your arms, move around and finally open your eyes.

Use a notebook to record your fantasy games while they are still fresh in your mind. Write concisely, but include details. As part of the recording process, note your insights, then write an analysis of your experience. If you can do this simultaneously with another person and then share experiences, you'll both gain even more.

The Unmanifest World

There are many dimensions to the unmanifest world, for unmanifest simply means non-physical. We have discussed already the elementals of the natural world, the highly intelligent and powerful nature spirits who helped the members of the Findhorn community. Just as the natural world is populated with numerous "unseen" entities, so are the countless other realms that exist beyond, within and in conjunction with our known, physical world.

We are capable of developing our knowledge of these unmanifest worlds and communicating with the beings who reside there. Doing so will broaden our experience and bring us greater vitality, knowledge and power. It will make us happier, healthier and more prosperous. If we give up our limited views in favor of expanded awareness, our experience of life itself will be enhanced. If we believe there are supersensible worlds to discover, they will be revealed to us. We need only to ask, to seek, to knock and the doors will be opened to us.

The World of the Oversoul

Our higher selves are in contact with the world of the oversoul—the highest world of being. This is the plane of origin where each of us began and remains.

We often think of the "soul" as the part of us that is the eternal spark of Divine Mind, the god within, seeking its way back to its creator. For some, this realm represents potential still to be realized. It contains the key to one's destiny and purpose for physical existence. This world is the highest state of consciousness we can hope to gain, and gaining wisdom of this higher realm is the objective all our selves must serve.

Many people believe that this spiritual dimension is the place where our guides live. Spirit guides are entities who oversee our progress in the physical world and offer guidance to us. Some people think of them as their protective ancestors. Others view their guides as guardian angels. Whoever they are, these higher beings can be contacted and known. They are always there to help us— whether or not we realize it. By becoming attuned to the wisdom they offer us, we can improve the quality of our lives immeasurably. Individuals who do so are sometimes said to lead a "charmed life," but they simply have learned to live in harmony with the Universal Will and to accept guidance from this source of universal wisdom.

Fantasy game "Your spirit guide": This fantasy game is based on the premise that relationships are possible with discarnate beings—angels, devas, ancestors, teachers and guides—using the technique of telepathic communication. This game can help when you need guidance in making choices and decisions, and setting goals. Have a friend read the following script to you, or pre-record it yourself on tape.

In a quiet, private place, relax your physical body and your conscious self. As your physical body becomes limp and comfortable, allow your conscious mind to drop the cares of the day. You find yourself in a beautiful meadow—a meadow filled with the sights, sounds and smells of a lovely summer day. The sun is warm on your skin, the murmur of a nearby brook lulls you and the breezes caress you softly. You can smell the flowers and hear the hum of insects. A path stretches before you, leading to the edge of a small forest in the distance. These woods represent your desire and will emanate exactly what you need.

As you experience this scene, take the position of observer—don't try to bring about the next experience. Just allow it to happen to you. Remain quiet and relaxed, enjoying this fantasy which will remain clear in your mind for later analysis.

As you watch, your spirit guide steps out of the woods and walks toward you on the path. Allow this guide to be whatever it will. Allow it to emerge into your awareness without any assistance from you. Do not criticize or object to it. As your guide comes closer, become aware of its qualities, form and appearance. You may experience the particular essence of your guide as a scent or odor which can help you identify its presence in the future. Mentally ask its name and it will respond. The guide stops, facing you and you begin a telepathic communication with its mind. Ask questions and it will respond.

Go slow. Don't overdo your conversation at this time for you need to work at establishing a simple and valuable relationship. You may want to set up guidelines for working together—times, places and contexts which seem best for both of you. In the future you will meet your guide with a prepared agenda, but this introduction is for the purpose of becoming acquainted.

When you feel you have completed your aim, bid goodbye to your guide and thank it for being in your life. Let the guide either return to the forest or just disappear as you return to your normal awareness. Wiggle your toes, flex your legs and stretch your limbs like a cat waking from a nap. Open your eyes and resume your daily schedule.

The Underworld

The world of the oversoul contains many levels. One level is called the underworld. It is here that mythological figures reside in the universal consciousness. These mythic figures, such as gods and goddesses, have been created by humankind as a sort of group projection or mass thought form. They exist for us in the underworld, and even though our conscious selves might not have experienced them, our higher selves know them well.

Here also exist our archetypes, what psychiatrist C. G. Jung described as thought forms or ideas derived from the collective experience of a racial group which reside in the individual unconscious. We respond to these unconscious archetypes or symbols—whether or not we recognize their existence—and often they form the basis of our expectations. For example, Western society's collective experience of God instills in each Western individual an archetypal "god" against which any personal experience is measured. The same is true for archetypes such as mother, father, man, woman, etc. Archetypes frequently are depicted as characters in plays, paintings, songs and poems.

Each "group" of which you are a member has its own set of archetypes. Thus your unconscious contains archetypal images that relate to your religion's collective experiences, your country's, your family's, etc. Usually we are unaware of the archetypes we respond to and how they influence our attitudes and behavior. Here is a technique for recognizing some of the symbolic beings who reside in your personal unconscious, in your underworld.

Tarot exercise for understanding archetypes: This exercise helps you to discover the "people" and concepts that influence you at a deep, unconscious level. Since the unconscious understands the language of pictures and symbols, you can effectively use Tarot cards to communicate with it. It doesn't matter which of the many decks you use; work with the one you feel most comfortable with or like best.

Begin by looking through the deck and selecting a card that you feel represents you at this time. This is called the significator. Though many Tarot readers use a queen (or other female card such as the High Priestess) for a woman and a king (or other male card) for a man, you need not limit yourself in this exercise. Now pick a card to represent each archetype you wish to examine at this time: man, woman, mother, father, child, husband, wife, god, goddess, devil, leader, homeland, etc.

Next, determine which archetype you wish to understand first and place its card beside the card which symbolizes you. Look at the two cards together. What is happening in each card? How do you feel about each of them? What do you especially like/dislike about each? How do they relate to each other? Are there similarities between them? Does any color(s) predominate? Does one card call your attention to it more strongly than the other? Imagine them having a conversation; what do they say to each other? It is helpful to write down your thoughts and feelings, both to trigger your unconscious impressions and so you'll remember them later.

Repeat this process for each archetype you wish to explore. When you've considered each card along side the significator, place all of them together and look at them as a group. How do they relate to each other? Which ones seem to demand your attention? Which cards seem more important or more powerful; which seem less important or weaker? Do they get along with each other or are there tensions between them? Do any colors, numbers, symbols, suits (swords, wands/rods, pentacles/coins, cups) predominate? Are there any other noteworthy features in the cards, for instance, are all the figures looking straight at you or all looking away from you? Do any of the cards have anything to say to the others? Examine your feelings about these questions and your responses, and write them down for future reference.

If you feel you want to delve deeper into the meaning of one particular archetype, take time now to do so. You also can use this exercise to explore your unconscious responses to qualities such as loyalty, strength, compassion, love, hate, fear, sorrow, honesty, success, failure, courage, guilt. Over time, you might find that your understanding of these archetypal figures and your relationship with them changes. Thus, it is interesting to do this exercise once or twice a year and compare your responses.

Trance States

In a trance state, you shift from the masculine mode of functioning with your will and intellect, to a feminine mode of acute receptivity. When in a trance, you are observant, aware and receptive to all incoming information. Your will to act independently and your critical faculties are in abeyance, but can be aroused if you sense any threat or offense from your external environment. Sometimes you may drop into lower levels of consciousness and experience memories that are not available to your ordinary consciousness, though you probably won't bring those memories back with you when you return to normal waking awareness.

External conditions can impose trance states on us. Hypnosis, either self-induced or induced by another, is one way to bring on a trance state. Rhythmic sounds or patterns also can cause a trance since they affect brainwaves. Drivers sometimes go into involuntary hyponotic trances as a result of seeing rhythmic patterns of fence posts, trees or snow flurries.

Voluntary trances can be quite useful as a tool for self-understanding and personal growth, giving your awareness access to levels of consciousness normally barred from your experience.

Channeling

An increasingly popular phenomena called channeling is actually a revival of trance mediumship. What used to be known as a *medium* is now called a *channel*, a title commonly associated with the Spiritualist religion.

The dictionary defines a channel as a means of communication, a path along which information flows. In this case, a medium is a "channel" of communication between the earthly world and a world of spirits. Currently, the label "channel" is given to a person who brings forth, in writing or speech, material which s/he classifies as coming from entities outside his/her own energy field or consciousness.

Discarnate entities (entities who do not have physical bodies) take over the channel's physical functions, speech, body language, emotional and cognitive expression for a time. The person acting as the channel temporarily abdicates his or her physical body and willingly loans it to the disincarnate entity.

The purpose of channeling is to provide a vehicle for communications from another reality to occur in this one. Often the messages communicated through a trance medium or channel offer insight into life after death. Sometimes a departed entity will contact family or friends who are still in the physical world. Other entities, such as the one known as Seth who speaks through writer Jane Roberts, bring messages for all humankind. Channeling confirms the continuation of the spirit after the death of the physical body.

Throughout history, individuals have channeled material from disembodied spirits. When we review that history, it is interesting to note that those people who channeled the most enlightening ideas were reluctant to perform when contacted by invisible spirits. Mediumship entered their lives unbidden, and in many cases, unwanted. This factor may seem insignificant, but it is a clue to what we find happening today. We all need guidelines to help us separate the wheat from the chaff, the nourishing from the garbage. Of course our own discrimination, if developed, will help us evaluate the material so we will not be unduly impressed by the source. But more concrete guidelines are available, too, and we can utilize them.

Good communication requires a clear line—a clear channel which is not distorted by a lot of pre-conceptions, fears and beliefs. If a telephone line has a lot of static, for example, it is hard to understand the voice at the other end. The only people who can transmit ideas outside of their own minds successfully must have "empty" minds, or ones in which the egoic structures can be totally tranquilized during the transmission.

Because egoic contents of consciousness seek expression to satisfy egoic needs such as self-aggrandizement, channeling has great appeal. The conscious self is easily conned into believing the material entering awareness is from an outside source. The more widely recognized channeling becomes, the more egos will want to get into the act!

Here is our second clue. Individuals who seek to be channels are not the unwilling, reluctant objects of appeal from higher sources. It is possible, of course, that higher sources (than the channel) might use them as communicators, but I personally feel it is unlikely.

True channels are not responsible for the ideas expressed. Many are not even aware when the channeling takes place. Channels Madame Blavatsky and Alice Bailey, who very reluctantly took on the arduous task of translating the ideas of the Masters into material for public consumption, found it very difficult not to "contaminate" the expressions with their own ideas and beliefs. Jane Roberts' mediumship proved itself by the quality of the material, not by the phenomena of channeling (which can be quite impressive).

In one way or another, each channel must take responsibility for what issues from his or her mind. Channels should be aware of what lies in their own unconscious minds and be able to keep this from contaminating the flow of thought. Channels should examine their own material to see if it reflects any cultural or religious beliefs, personal value systems or morality.

Many levels of intelligence, from the most ignorant to the most wise, exist in the invisible realms. Many deceased individuals still remain wrapped in cultural sheaths, identifying with a religion, race or society. Communication with humankind on earth is not the province of highly evolved entities only; beings of all levels seek to contact us. Within the limits of their expertise on earth, their advice can be listened to with benefit— but only to the extent you would honor it if they were here in the flesh, physically speaking or writing to you.

All entities communicating from their personal, past-life identities must be viewed in the context of that life, and their biases and prejudices recognized as such.

How does one benefit from channeling? By developing the same kind of discrimination in that area that we use to choose our most intimate friends. Channels should not merely perpetuate outworn philisophy and empty rhetoric. All channeled material should make us feel better, more positive, more knowledgable. We should feel more secure, not less. More confident, not less so.

What is egoic channeling? The prophets of doom and gloom are egoic. The ones who instill fear and trembling are egoic. The ones who preach religiously and morally are egoic.

To determine the value of channeled information, abstract from it the essential message. Write that message down coherently or express it understandably to a friend. If you cannot explain what you felt was trans- mitted except in vagaries, it had little value.

In this country we often put emphasis on the source instead of the product. We look for identity, title and reputation as verifiers of worth. *Who* is more important than *what.* Who said it, we ask, rather than what was said. I feel all channeling should stand on its own merits, and all identity-authority should be eliminated. A name should only serve to designate the author. Notably, some of the best in recent years have used names with no authority quality—Seth, Mentor and Lazaris, for instance.

Mental Mediumship

The practice of mental mediumship does not involve the process of abdicating the physical body and allowing another entity to use it. Rather, it requires developing your own subtle sense organs so you can experience other realities. These subtle sense organs, which parallel the physical sense organs of sight, hearing, smell, taste and touch, are normally inactive. On occasion, a subtle sense organ can become active spontaneously and allow a momentary experience of another reality. However, purposely activating these subtle sense organs is a demanding process that requires much skill, persistence and practice.

Meditation

With the right training, this state of consciousness can be achieved by anyone. Most people can meditate without any instruction at all. Meditation is a state of physical and mental relaxation in which respiration, pulse and brainwave activity are slowed. There are countless methods for inducing this state, some already have been described in this book.

One of the best-known methods is called Transcendental Meditation or simply TM. This method gained acceptance in the medical community after Dr. Herbert Benson researched the physiological and psychological effects of meditation on patients and reported his findings in his book *The Relaxation Response*.[4] Benson found that TM alleviated stress, lowered blood pressure and heart rate, and was beneficial for his patients. In TM, one chants or repeats a *mantra* (a special word or sound) to lull the mind into a quiet, receptive mood. Meditation helps provide inner quiet and give us a break from the mental activity and stress we experience in our everyday lives.

Quieting the inner self: Begin by explaining to your inner self that meditation is a state both of you will benefit from and enjoy. Tell your inner self that you will give it your complete attention for a period so it can communicate to you anything it wishes to express, after which you would like its cooperation in establishing a period of quiet. Make sure you have writing materials nearby so you can record any communication from your inner self. Once you have received messages from your inner self, tell it you will consider these communications after completing the meditation period. Invite your inner self to quietly participate in your meditation.

If your inner self is overexcited and has difficulty calming down, use a word or phrase that is soothing when repeated as a sort of lullaby. Or, you may choose to sing silently a simple phrase that conveys tranquility, such as "peace to all." Experience the emotions of comfort and caring as you sound the word or phrase you have chosen. Use the same word or phrase each time you begin meditation so it becomes a trigger for your inner self to induce this quiet, relaxed state. Eventually just the thought of the word or phrase will bring about a meditative state and you'll be able to use it whenever you want to calm anxiety or fears.

Meditating on a regular basis for periods of about fifteen minutes at a time can improve mental and physical health, increase energy and provide an overall sense of well-being. It also is a tool to actualize more of your potential, achieve greater personal harmony, solve daily problems and encounter new experiences in consciousness.

Meditation technique: Choose a time and place where you can be comfortable, quiet and undisturbed. Relax using one of the breathing methods described earlier. You may wish to touch your thumbs and index fingers together or fold your hands. Start sounding silently within your head, a "mantra" or word or phrase. "OM" is a popular sound, but you can use anything you wish. (I like to repeat the numeral "one".)

Decide that you will sound your word for a specified amount of time; I recommend starting with a three-minute period and lengthening it as you become more skillful or want to enjoy a longer period. For your first three-minute meditation, give your inner self the task of arousing you in three minutes, then begin silently chanting "one." If your mind wanders, change your chant to "two." Every time your mind wanders, change the number. What number are you on at the end of three minutes? This method reveals your current ability to focus your attention. As you grow more proficient, you'll find yourself staying with lower numbers and thus can measure your increased skill.

Contemplation

Comtemplation is a form of meditation during which a thought, idea or concept is explored in depth. Proverbs, sayings and symbols are often the basis of a contemplative meditation. In contemplation, you focus on your chosen idea for the duration of the meditation without drifting into other thoughts. The goal is to consider first its most apparent meanings, then, like peeling away an onion skin, to see through its transparencies into the depths below.

While contemplating a symbol or thought, it is helpful to notice your distractions, since these may provide insights later. Consider the thought both as a unit and as a composition of individual words. Try as many different approaches as possible to help you in your analysis and understanding. The purpose of contemplation is to achieve insight and deeper knowledge of an idea or symbol.

Subjects for contemplation: You may have heard about Eastern mystics contemplating the sound of one hand clapping. Monks, nuns and other religious persons frequently contemplate verses of scripture to gain deeper insight into the meaning "between the lines."

You may find it helpful to contemplate the symbol for your astrological sign (consult a book on astrology if you are unfamiliar with what yours looks like) or the wheel of your birth chart. A Tarot card—one drawn randomly from the deck, one that you have designated already as your significator, or simply one that attracts your attention—is another good subject for contemplation. A hexagram from the *I Ching* may be used, too. Religious symbols or objects, such as a cross, Star of David or pentacle, often are contemplated. Crystals or other gemstones are also good choices. So are passages from esoteric literature, some proverbs, myths, sayings, fairy tales, dream images, musical notes, even certain words, such as love, truth, power, beauty, justice and independence. Subjects for contemplation may be pictorial symbols, written or spoken words, non-representational sounds, even physical objects. The possibilities are endless.

Notes

1. Rudolf Steiner, *Knowledge of the Higher Worlds and Its Attainment* (New York: Anthroposophic Press, Inc., 1947), pp. 50–52.

2. J. Allen Boone, *The Language of Silence* (New York: Harper & Row, Publishers, Inc., 1970).

3. Peter Tompkins and Christopher Bird, *The Secret Life of Plants* (New York: Avon Books, 1973), pp. 19–26.

4. Herbert Benson, M.D., *The Relaxation Response* (New York: William Morrow and Co., Inc., 1975).

4

Expanding Creative Skills

Ask any athlete how important concentration is to playing well. Unless you focus your attention completely, you won't be able to bat the ball, jump the hurdle or hit the bullseye with any degree of success. The same is true for each of us in our daily lives. The ability to focus attention on a goal is the key to success in any endeavor.

Attention is the power behind imagination, and imagination is the source of creation. If you can imagine a result, visualize it in your mind's eye and concentrate your attention fully on that visualization, you can make it happen.

Developing your capacity to focus and control your attention involves training your ego to stop interfering. The ego carries on a continual commentary in your mind which distracts and diffuses attention. Most of us so rarely experience direct attention—that which is not accompanied by thinking and analyzing—we don't even realize it exists.

Just like the athlete, you can learn to focus your attention so that it is like a magnifying glass concentrating light rays into a single, powerful beam. The better your control, the clearer your visualizations will be and the more power you'll have to affect changes in your life. It isn't difficult unless you believe it is. All it requires is the right technique, feeling, intention—and practice.

Attention

Attention energizes and activates whatever it touches. It is like a flashlight shining in a dark forest. The tree which is the flashlight's target receives the light of its energy. Like the flashlight beam, your energy flows toward the target you've chosen. The natural self follows and mirrors the action of the conscious self, combining its energy with that of the conscious self to make a connection between you and the focus of your attention. The target responds to the extent of your ability to transmit intention, feeling and energy. Like the flashlight, if your batteries are strong the light will shine brightly against the target. But, if your batteries of intention are weak, the beam of projected light will be barely noticeable. What you picture clearly and give energy to will become reality to the extent of your creative abilities.

Attention focusing experiment: You can see the effects of your focused attention by trying this experiment. The next time you are in a theater, a crowded bus, a restaurant or other public place, select one person in the group and focus your gaze on him/her. Let your attention flow outward, toward that individual. Before long, this person will feel your attention and look for its source. How quickly your "target" responds will depend upon your ability to focus your attention and your subject's sensitivity.

Attention is the vehicle for the transmission of essential life energy. Wherever attention goes energy flows. This vital life energy is generated within each one of us and we support each other in our survival by exchanging it. Each animate being is a generator of life energy, transmitting that energy along the line of focused attention. None of us can survive physically, socially or spiritually without this support from our fellow creatures.

Getting and Giving Attention

Attention. We need to get it, we are capable of giving it and we all enjoy exchanging it with other animate creatures. This is part of the plan of creation itself.

Take a moment to recall some experience of an exchange of attention between yourself and an animal pet—a dog or cat, perhaps a horse, hampster or parakeet. Close your eyes and let the memory become vivid. The flow of attention energy had specific feeling qualities that related to the circumstances of the exchange. As you remember, think of the particular qualities of that energy and your response to the experience. Continue remembering experiences of getting attention. Mentally explore the kinds of attention you have received from other human beings. Which did you like and which repelled you?

At a conference I attended recently, I met a man who constantly used behavior that irritated others. He got their attention by being late for every event he attended, and by taking advantage of those who were socially conditioned to be "polite." His demands for attention were frequent and annoying. Of course, his attempts were not really successful; most people tried to avoid him whenever possible. He needed attention desperately, but lacked skills in exchanging it or attracting it.

Get out your notebook and head a page with MY BELIEFS ABOUT ATTENTION. Describe ways you use your attention. Do you listen fully when others talk or are you thinking of your next response? Does your attention leap quickly from one object or thought to another? How long can you hold your attention on one idea? List your experience with attention. Have you ever been sated with attention? Do you often feel deprived of attention or in need of it? Have you ever felt smothered from too much attention? What are some of the methods you've developed to get attention? Are they successful? Have they elicited the kind of attention you desire? Keeping this notebook for review from time to time will allow you to see the changes in your attitudes and practices involving attention.

Attention and Concentration

Attention can be focused fully or partially, intensely or slightly. Most of us operate with a "divided mind." We divide our attention between several things and it is sometimes difficult for us to focus completely on one at a time. For example, you may be engaged in conversation with someone but your attention drifts off in other directions. Divided attention sends only a small amount of energy toward a target and has little effect on anyone or the environment.

Attention is a faculty of awareness; consciousness perceives the whole. As a result, awareness pays attention to the foreground while consciousness assesses the background. If you are talking with someone, your attention may be on what that person is saying while your consciousness is observing the rest of the environment.

If you focus on a person's outward appearance, your awareness will only reach that far. This limitation is helpful in one sense because it keeps you from being overwhelmed. However, we should realize the limitations of our perception and *choose* the extent of our focus. Sometimes it may be enough to focus on another's outward appearance only. At other times, it may be important to understand what's going on beneath the surface. If you want to know how someone else feels, all you have to do is focus your attention there and you will become aware of that person's inner experience.

Through developing your attention and sensitivity to receiving it from others, you will increase your ability to connect with loved ones whenever you choose, no matter how far apart you are. Through the vehicle of attention, you can communicate over great distances, instantaneously. Have you ever been thinking about someone and suddenly gotten a phone call from that person— even though months or years had elapsed since you last spoke together? This is an example of focused attention.

Attention exercise: Listen to a recording of orchestral music. Begin by choosing one instrument you want to hear distinctly from the others, perhaps a trumpet, violin or drum. Listen to it intently, focusing your awareness on it. You will be able to distinguish every note clearly. Now switch to another instrument. Again, you will hear the notes of that instrument above the rest— the other notes will become background to the instrument you have chosen. Continue switching instruments, listening to each separately from the others. You'll discover that your new skill also will allow you to hear one selected voice clearly even at a noisy, crowded party!

When attention is focused on a subject so intently that the background seems to disappear entirely, you are in a state of concentration. Concentration is the ability to completely immerse yourself in something to the exclusion of all else, and to stay with it through all its changing states.

Through the use of focused attention, you are expanding your channels of communication. Through these opened channels, you can get at information that was previously beyond your scope. Using the power inherent in focused attention, you can begin to perceive on many different levels of reality. You can perform mental magic—recalling lost memories, influencing your other selves and communicating with other people on new levels.

Daydreaming

When you daydream, you are actually focusing attention inwardly. In so doing, you experience an altered state of consciousness. This passive awareness with its flow of images and ideas often is triggered by the subconscious mind. But, daydreaming is not always a passive experience—it can involve active thinking as well. Awareness may direct the daydream in specific areas. Daydreaming can be fun and pleasurable, or it can release thoughts and feelings of fear, anger, sadness.

Daydreaming is a way of seeking stimulation inside ourselves. Psychologists call a person who looks inward for stimulation an introvert, and one who looks to the outer world for stimulation an extrovert. Are you an extrovert or introvert? Try this experiment with the pendulum and see for yourself.

Pendulum exercise: Draw a semi-circle on a piece of paper. Label the left side "introvert" and the right side "extrovert." Call the middle "neutral." Ask the pendulum to swing in the direction of your predominance.

You also may ask the pendulum to indicate the degree of your predominance; it will respond by swinging far to the right if you are extremely extroverted, just barely into the left hemisphere if you are slightly introverted. For insight into how you compare to others, ask your friends to "dowse" their tendencies, too.

Either extreme can be harmful. People who are overly dependent on external stimulation because they lack internal stimulation can turn to coffee, alcohol, drugs, cigarettes, food addictions or other artificial stimulants. Those who are overly dependent on internal stimulation may become so lost in their own fantasies that they stop relating to the outside world at all.

Attention and Attitude

Our attitudes greatly influence the path our attention takes. Some people, for example, will see a glass of water as half full while others perceive it as half empty. If you find that your attention is always drawn to what's wrong or unpleasant in the world, you probably suffer from "half-empty" syndrome. Your negative attitude is directing your attention to all the places that support this pessimistic viewpoint. If, however, you usually notice the joyful, positive aspects of your world, you fall into the "half-full" category. While it may not be desireable to maintain a "pollyanna" attitude, you will feel better if you look at the lighter, brighter, hopeful side of life than if you are always focusing your attention on the world's ills.

Redirecting your attention: You can change your attitude and your life by redirecting your attention. Look at nature. Observe the plants and animals, even those you usually take for granted like the neighborhood maple tree or a pigeon in the park. Watch the sunset or sunrise. Marvel at the complex beauty of a flower. Another way to begin changing your focus to the more positive side is to note in your journal what is right in your life. Every day, jot down something good that transpired—the beautiful weather, a co-worker's compliment, an unexpected invitation, a bargain at the supermarket.

All thoughts and feelings have creative power since they influence the inner self to make them manifest in the physical world. Our inner selves are constantly creating the world in our images. Therefore, if you focus on the negative, your inner self will try to create unpleasant situations to carry out your intent. Conversely, if you direct your attention to the positive things around you, you'll encourage your inner self to create more happy, satisfying experiences for you to enjoy.

Visualization

Because the inner self thinks and perceives through imagery, it is influenced most strongly by pictures. You can use images and imagery purposefully to influence and guide your inner self. Many times we unwittingly give our inner selves images that work to create mishaps, accidents or illness. Worrying about being in a car accident and continually envisioning a collision in your mind, for instance, eventually can bring it about.

A psychic once told me, "You have a heavy foot on the gas pedal. You are going to get in trouble with that." Although I told myself her statement was inaccurate, I am easily programmed and two days later I got a speeding ticket which fulfilled her prophecy.

We can use visualization to program ourselves in countless ways: to develop a new skill or improve an existing one; to change a relationship or attract a new one; to erase an old attitude and replace it with a new one. We can plant the harvest of our future with the seeds of our imaginations.

Visualization is an activity of the aware mind. With this technique you can give yourself commands, orders or goals to be reached.

Painting the Perfect Picture

Your visualizations will be more effective if you create them when you are quiet, relaxed and in a state of consciousness where your inner self is paying attention to you. One of the best ways to get the attention of your inner self is to control your breathing, changing it from an involuntary process to a voluntary one. Use any breathing exercise or technique you want, then when you are relaxed, you can return to your normal breathing pattern.

As we've discussed before, your inner self interprets directions literally. Therefore, you program it by visualizing a picture or symbol and accompanying that image with a clear statement, or *affirmation*, of your intention. Be sure your visualization and intention aren't ambiguous. Your inner self also responds better to active pictures than to still images. The feelings that you experience during such an exercise are important, too, since they "color" the picture. You can even use colors to intensify and reinforce your visualization.

It is not enough simply to visualize a result and expect that it will happen. Very often, even though we desire something at a conscious level, we may want the opposite at an unconscious level. This conflict confuses or nullifies the visualizations. Perhaps you wish to reduce your weight and visualize yourself twenty pounds lighter. But if you have been programmed from childhood to "eat up" so you'll be healthy, you'll have two opposing ideas working against each other. The earlier programming will override the later visualization if it has been reinforced more often. How can you know if your visualization is in conflict with other programming, beliefs or ideas? Ask your inner self for that answer.

Before creating your visualization, examine it carefully. Is it worthwhile? To whom? Who might lose from the actualization of your visualization? If what you want will benefit others, you will have the cooperation of all the unconscious levels of those others. Your higher self will help rather than hinder you when everyone stands to gain from your future vision. It will not assist you, however, in any endeavor that would harm another.

Before you begin visualizing, be sure that the result is one you really want. Remember the saying: "Be careful what you ask for because you may just get it."

Once you have a design that suits you perfectly and you are certain you want to see it actualized, you are ready to contact your inner self and ask whether there are any barriers to this result. Sit quietly. Focus your attention on your inner self and communicate your proposed visualization.

Ask your inner self to reveal any opposition. You may sense a feeling of "go ahead" and if so, you can feel confident about proceeding. If, however, you sense that you should change your design, do so. If you do not receive enough information you can use your pendulum. Once you have gained the information you need, you can proceed or redesign your visualization as necessary.

Visualization technique:

1. Choose a place and time when you will be alone and undisturbed.

2. Begin breathing slowly, deeply, deliberately.

3. Reopen your level of relaxation and concentration by counting down slowly from ten to one, pausing to focus on each number before moving to the next. Or, you may imagine the colors of the spectrum in order, from red to violet, focusing your mind's eye on each color in turn until it is clear and vivid.

4. Make sure *you* are in the visualization. Otherwise, you may not be part of the action when it happens!

5. Envision every detail of your picture vividly. Keep in mind your deep desire to see this become actual. Keep feelings of happiness, joy and love strong during this process. See yourself in the visualization acting out the reality you desire.

Some people find visualization difficult at first. One way you can "prime" your imagination and train your visualization skills is to use the following technique which I use as an introduction to fantasy games. Relax, take your time and observe what comes into your mind without judging, evaluating or analyzing the images. Allow your imagination free rein. Let yourself experience the emotions that arise to accompany your visualizations. You may find it helpful to make a tape recording of this process and play it to yourself.

Fantasy game introduction "The meadow": As you sit quietly, relaxed, with your eyes closed, imagine that you are in a darkened room, like a movie theatre, with a blank screen in front of you. On that screen appears a picture of a rose. What color is it? Is it a bud or in full flower? Now see the stem, leaves and thorns. As you watch, a gentle breeze causes the rose to sway slightly. Inhale deeply. You can smell the rose. Its scent is distinct, rich and refreshing. Do you experience any emotion connected with this image?

Continue watching the rose, but now you notice that it is only one flower among many in a beautiful meadow. The screen in front of you shows a lovely country vista with soft green grass, dozens of different colored flowers, mountains in the distance and a blue sky overhead. Butterflies dart between the flowers. You can hear bees humming as they go about their work, flitting from flower to flower. Listen to their buzzing. Continue listening and you notice birds singing. Hear one bird call to another, hear the second bird answer. Pay attention to any feelings that arise with this image.

See yourself standing in the green meadow. You are barefoot and the grass is warm and soft beneath your feet. Begin walking slowly through the meadow, enjoying the touch of the grass on your skin. The sun is warm overhead and you can feel it on your head, your neck, your shoulders, your arms. Now you are approaching a tumbling brook that runs through the meadow. As you near it, you can hear the water cascading over rocks in the stream bed. The water is blue and clear and you can see to the bottom of the stream. Sit at the edge of the brook and dip your feet in its cool water. Feel the water rippling around your feet and ankles, tickling your toes, caressing your skin. Inhale and smell the cool, refreshing air around you. Let any emotions associated with this experience arise in you.

Now gradually let the scene fade. Slowly return to the dark movie theatre, and imagine yourself seated before a blank screen. Gently wiggle your feet and hands, then open your eyes.

Visualization exercise: As you sit quietly, comfortable and relaxed, with your eyes closed, imagine yourself standing just inside the front door of your house. See the door. What color is it? Now reach for the doorknob. Feel the coolness of the knob as you close your hand around it. Turn the knob and swing the door open. Just outside, parked at the curb in front of your house is an automobile. What color is it? Notice the make, style and condition of the car. Is it clean and shiny, or dusty and mud-splattered? Is it new, or old and dented? A sedan, convertible or station wagon? What features catch your attention? Walk all the way around the car, observing every detail. Look at the roof, the tires, the windows, the bumpers, the grill.

Now open the front left door and get into the driver's seat. See the interior of the car. What color is it? What material is used for the upholstery? Feel the fabric with your hands. See the dash panel in detail, the gauges, lights, dials. Does the car have a clock? A radio? What other special features or gadgets are there?

Place your hands on the steering wheel. Feel your fingers close around the wheel. Now turn the key in the ignition and start the car. Listen to the motor; is it smooth and quiet, or noisy, irregular, complaining? Press your foot on the accelerator and feel yourself take command of the vehicle.

How do you feel about being in charge of the car? Are you confident or apprehensive? What other feelings arise in connection with this experience of driving?

Pull away from the curb and begin driving. See the road in front of you. Are there other cars on the road? Is this a narrow country road, a city street, a busy multi-lane highway? A familiar route or one that is new to you? What signs do you see along the way? Are there trees? Buildings? Let your imagination take in everything as you continue driving. Is it day or night? Sunny, cloudy, raining, snowing? Experience the sensation of movement, the vibration of the vehicle beneath your body, the rumbling of the engine.

Now see an exit or road leading off the one on which you have been driving. Turn onto it and start back home. Visualize your own street, then watch as your house comes into view. Pull the car up to the curb once more and turn off the ignition. Sit quietly and let the image of the car's interior fade away. Gently wiggle your feet and hands, then slowly open your eyes.

You can use visualizations to attract a new relationship, find a job, improve a skill, receive money, heal an injury, and to succeed in countless other ways. Remember as you design your visualization that you will have to accept and live with the results. For example, if you visualize yourself owning an expensive new car, you will have to accept the payments, insurance and upkeep that go along with it. Think very carefully about the consequences and responsibilities of your visualizations and design your visualizations meticulously.

Imagination

Using Your Imagination

A friend of mine is a concert pianist. Whenever he has difficulty with a new piece of music, he uses his imagination to help smooth out the rough spots and improve his playing. In his mind he visualizes his hands, in slow motion, moving over the piano keys, performing with perfect rhythm and technique. Over and over, he rehearses the sequences in his imagination, gradually increasing his tempo until finally he is able to play the new piece perfectly in his imagination. He then is able to transfer his visualization to a physical result.

My friend has learned that practicing mentally can enhance his physical skill. Rehearsing in your imagination repeats the "picture" again and again until it becomes an automatic response for your inner self. You can use this technique to improve your golf game, to ace an exam or to land a job.

Technique for getting a job: Focus on the end result. If your goal is landing a job, do not imagine yourself merely interviewing for it. Your visualization should be a picture of yourself performing the job, happily and confidently. You also may want to examine this visualization to determine what traits, skills or personality characteristics you'll need to perform the job optimally and be content in it. Then make a list of these traits, skills, etc., and give them to your inner self to develop. Visualize yourself already possessing them and your inner self will work to accomplish your goal.

Before you begin, ask you inner self if it is in agreement with this goal. If not, it will oppose you and orchestrate your failure. If you do not get a prompt, clear answer from your inner self, use your pendulum to dowse for the answer.

If you have trouble visualizing yourself as you would like to be, the following exercises can help.

Exercise #1: Sit quietly, relax and close your eyes. Choose a trait—compassion, humor, courage, intelligence, patience—that you wish to project. Now bring to mind someone who displays that inner quality. It can be a friend, a co-worker, a religious or political figure, even an actor portraying that quality in a movie role. Watch how s/he moves, speaks and acts. Now picture yourself displaying that quality in situations where it is important. Keep rehearsing until you are able to project the quality in a natural and comfortable way.

Exercise #2: Another way to convey your intentions to your inner self is to post pictures which illustrate your objectives in a place where you will see them frequently. Use photographs or magazine pictures to represent your goals. If you want to get a job, display photos of someone performing that job. Write your name on the figure in the picture or cut out your face from another photograph and paste it on the model. The same technique can be used if your goal is to lose weight, buy a new house, take a vacation or win a tennis tournament. Simply find pictures which clearly illustrate your intention to plant the seed in your imagination.

Exercise for losing weight: New York psychiatrist Dr. Jack Leedy recognized the potential of imagination in losing weight and created a weight-reducing program that involved imagination. In his book, *How To Eat Like a Thin Person*, Leedy says some patients lost as much as one hundred pounds on this diet, without feeling hungry, deprived or guilty.[1]

The key is to indulge yourself in your imagination while actually eating a healthy, low-calorie diet. At the first sign of hunger sit down, relax and close your eyes. Begin planning a menu of the foods you most enjoy. Imagine how they would look attractively displayed on your table. Smell the delicious aroma. Help yourself to as much as you want and begin eating, savoring each bite. Pay attention to every detail of this experience. Mentally chew each mouthful slowly and eat until your plate is empty. Now, without any guilt, serve yourself a second or even a third helping. Really live the experience. When you feel satisfied, visualize yourself getting up from the table. You will be amazed to find your hunger and desire for food are gone.

This fantasy communicates to your subconscious mind that you have had enough to eat. You will experience the same sensations as if you actually had eaten food—relaxation, contentment and a full stomach. At mealtime, you'll find you are able to eat a light but nutritious meal that helps you lose weight without feeling deprived.

Weight loss technique: One of the problems with most diets is that a lot of time and mental effort are spent obsessing about food. Many diets even require listing foods that can and cannot be eaten. A great deal of attention is spent thinking about those forbidden foods and the inner self interprets this attention as a desire.

To help your inner self produce the results you want, use the "picture" method discussed above. From magazines, cut out pictures of bodies that look the way you want yours to look and paste them on a piece of poster board or cardboard. Next, paste photos of your face on the necks of those bodies. Or, if you once were the size and shape you'd like to be again, paste photos of the thinner you on your picture board. You also might include words or phrases like "slim and trim" or "my perfect body" or "I am beautiful" to reinforce the image. Looking at these pictures frequently will help get the point across to your inner self.

Color

Color affects our moods, our emotions and our energy. Decorators and marketing people utilize color to influence the public—to make us feel cozy, hungry or relaxed. Business offices are usually decorated in greys, tans, blues or greens so that the colors do not distract workers. Restaurants often use reds and oranges to stimulate hunger.

You, too, can make use of color and its inherent power. Color can add another dimension to your visualizations because each color has its own, unique qualities. Light—the unbroken spectrum of color—is actually life and feeling. When light is broken into its components, it represents all the different tones of feeling which we are capable of experiencing.

Primary or "pure" colors—red, blue and yellow—cannot be created from other colors. Secondary or "blended" colors are combinations of two pure colors: green is actually yellow-blue, orange is yellow-red and purple is red-blue.

Colors also can be considered positive, negative or neutral. Red is a positive color, meaning it engenders active, outer-directed feelings in us when we look at it. When a panel or wall is painted red, it seems to be advancing toward the viewer. By contrast, blue is a negative color. It creates passive, inner-directed feelings in us. A blue wall will appear to be receding from the viewer. The third pure color, yellow, is neutral and takes on the qualities of whichever color is mixed with it. Green (or yellow-blue) is negative, orange (or yellow-red) is positive.

Positive colors are powerful, controlling, dominating. Red is easily recognized as a color which will STOP your motion, for example. It demands your attention and controls it. Positive colors also are arousing, stimulating, exciting. Red can be used to stimulate passion, to enrage or to counteract depression and weakness.

Negative colors are matrix colors and, like alkaline, furnish the force for growth and expansion. Matrix (negative) colors have a feminine, maternal quality, nurturing growth and productivity. Notice how often the figure of Mary, mother of Jesus, appears in blue robes in Christian symbology. Negative colors tranquilize and give a sense of space. Test subjects usually underestimate the amount of the time they spend in blue or green rooms, and overestimate their stay in red or orange rooms.

Yellow, a neutral color, is unbiased and non-judgmental. It is the color of sunlight, sand, wheat, autumn leaves and many other "earthy" things. Pure yellow is helpful to any system which requires neutrality, including our nervous systems.

Each color has an opposite or complement, what I call the "other side" of that color. This is the color we don't ordinarily see, the invisible or unmanifest side of the visible color. For instance, purple (or violet) is the invisible or other side of yellow. Green is the other side of red, and orange is the other side of blue. When you mix any color with its opposite, you neutralize or nullify it; when you combine red paint with green paint, for example, the result is gray. These two aspects of a color can never be truly separated. The "other side of the rainbow" has all the colors we've ever seen and perhaps some we haven't!

Color exercise #1: This exercise lets you see the other side of colors. Stare at a piece of red paper for a few moments. Now look away, at a plain white surface. You'll see what's called an "after image," a faint greenish glow which is the complement of red. Try the same thing with a piece of blue paper. When you look at the white surface you'll see orange—the other side of blue. If you close your eyes, you also can see a color's after image on the backs of your eyelids.

Color exercise #2: Place a single-colored flower such as a yellow daffodil or a deep red rose in a vase. Set the vase on the table and sit facing it so that your eyes are a few feet away from the flower. Gaze at the flower and as you stare at it, allow yourself to perceive the "other side" of its color. If your flower is yellow you'll soon notice a velvety purple aura or halo around it. If the flower is red, the aura you see will be green. Orange flowers have blue auras, purple flowers have yellow ones.

It is helpful to get a supply of paint chips from a paint store to use in your experiments. These can be your color guides. You also may want to purchase crayons or paints to use in creating color symbols for your exercises.

Pink

Fountain of youth exercise: Remember the expression "in the pink of health"? Sit in a place where you will be undisturbed and look at the paint chip you have selected. Close your eyes and look beyond the pink to the other side of pink—a lovely pale shade of green. Each color has two aspects, the invisible and visible, the external and internal. We can see this demonstrated in the leaves of a tree. They absorb the red rays of the light spectrum but display green to the outer world.

Once you have seen beyond pink to the green on the other side, let the green fade away and sit quietly. Now bring in all the energy from the Universe that will help increase your vitality. Imagine the area around you becoming a cloud of beautiful pink. Begin slowly to inhale this pink cloud, until it finally reaches the *Hara*, a point about two inches below your navel which is a center of energy and power. As you exhale, imagine pink light flooding your entire body, regenerating it. Continue breathing pink for several minutes. This exercise is a great way to start the day or as a refresher at work.

Let your love light shine: Lack of love may be responsible for may of the world's problems—crime, mental and physical illness, war. When we feel loved, we feel secure, confident, relaxed, at peace with ourselves and others. We are not angry or afraid. With this exercise, you can increase the amount of love in your environment and help counteract hostility and hatred.

Pink is often associated with love. Because of its love-related qualities, the color pink can help counteract anger and fear by bolstering self-love and esteem. Recall a time when you felt deeply loved and ask yourself what shade of pink that love felt like. Allow this shade of pink to come into your awareness; it is the love aspect of the total light spectrum.

You can begin to use this shade of pink to attract love and share love. You can send "love pink" energy to others on the wings of your attention, giving them the feeling of being loved. Simply by focusing your attention on someone and bathing him/her in the energy of pink light, you can give that person the gift of love.

In your mind, picture someone you feel could use a dose of love and imagine him or her surrounded by a cloud of love pink. Visualize this person absorbing the pink cloud—like a sponge soaking up water. See him/her become luminescent with the pink energy. As you send this love light, you, too, will experience the sensation of feeling loved.

You can use this same technique to increase your own supply of love. Begin with an affirmation such as: "We are all objects of Divine Love. That love is being poured out from the Source that supports the world and everything in it. Light contains love and love is the basis of life and growth. I experience pure love by removing the barriers within myself so that love energy can nurture me at the deepest levels of my consciousness."

After you recite this affirmation, close your eyes and imagine the cloud of love pink surrounding you. Imagine your body being porous, absorbing this energy through every pore. Your body pulses and glows with this marvelous pink energy of love.

The calming effect of pink: Bright, rosy pink has been used in a variety of behavioral experiments—from curbing appetite to reducing violence in prisons. The technique involves staring at a $3\frac{1}{2}'' \times 3\frac{1}{2}''$ square of bright pink, which sends a calming message to the brain.

To curb your appetite, sit in a quiet place and hold the pink square in front of you as if you were holding a book to read. As you look at the square, let your mind go blank. Relax and release all tension. After about five minutes, you will find that your urge to eat has diminished or faded entirely. The effects can last for two or three hours.

When placed in cells painted pink, even violent, angry inmates became calmer and more subdued. New prisoners who had been admitted through a pink reception area experienced the same effects. The presence of the color pink increased their sense of well-being and reduced their fear, thus lessening their inclinations to respond with violence.

Pink can bring serenity into your life, too, whenever you are agitated, tense or hostile. Choose the shade of pink that suggests to you a feeling of relaxation and calm. Close your eyes and imagine yourself wrapped in a blanket of this calming pink. You can help others to calm down, too, by visualizing them surrounded by this serene pink.

Blue

Blue has a calming, cleansing effect on us. Astringent and quieting, it is often called a "mental" color, for it can cool the emotions and allow clear mental reflection to take place. In excess, however, blue can create actual depression, what we call "the blues." Used in healing, blue acts as a purifier and an anesthetic. It also can help increase intuitive abilities.

White

One of the most powerful color visualizations uses white (actually clear) light, the light within which all color is contained. This white light energy has the ability to provide protection, to heal and to purify. You can visualize yourself or others surrounded by this white light. Imagine it shimmering and radiant with energy. When you surround yourself or others with this light you are projecting nurturing life energy. The great white light is Divine Love in its total essence.

Purple/Violet

This is the only secondary color in which neutral yellow is invisible. Yellow is actually purple's complement. When blue and red merge to become purple or violet, the result is simple power. The "royal purple" once worn by kings was an expression of this power. Subtle shades of violet are associated with spiritual power. Because yellow is the "other side" of purple, charismatic or powerful individuals usually have yellow auras around their heads; this effect is illustrated again and again in Early Christian paintings which show yellow halos around the heads of the Holy Family, angels, saints and other spiritual beings.

Violet is considered to be the dominant color of the New Age. It symbolizes the androgynous individual, deep purple the hermaphrodite. Violet is also the color of the centaur, deep purple the color of the Chthonic figure.

Purple's power to erase inauthentic forms and patterns created by egoic thinking is unsurpassed by any other color. Strong cultural paradigms that control our destinies can be transformed by the violet ray. The violet ray functions as a tester of the "real" or authentic, for only that which is real can survive its focused power.

In your visualizations, you can break down outdated or useless cultural preconceptions that are limiting your growth by focusing a beam of violet on yourself, or by "breathing" purple using the method described above for pink.

Black

Black has a magnetic quality, an ability to draw light to itself. It absorbs color because it has no light of its own. Astronomers are able to observe this situation when light approaches "black holes" in space and is absorbed. Black is the color of gravity.

"Holes" in one's energy field or aura are sometimes seen as black spots on an otherwise colored aura. These holes signify a loss of power. The great psychic Edgar Cayce once saw a group of people in an elevator that was about to crash. There were no auras at all around their heads— their power had already flown!

Gold and Silver

Gold and silver are complements, the "other side" of each other. Gold is a positive color, silver a negative one. We see these two depicted in the sun and moon. The golden sun is the light of day, warm, positive, masculine, creative. The silvery moon is the light of night, reflecting the sun's rays, cool, negative, feminine, regenerative. Silver is also the color of the *aka* cord, the thin, expandable thread of life substance that connects our physical and astral bodies.

Perception

Ralph Waldo Emerson put it succinctly when he said, "People only see what they are prepared to see." Our individual realities can only include what we can imagine. Our personal potential is bounded by our concepts of what is possible or probable. All of us want to know more, experience more and feel more. Expanding our perception—our way of seeing the world—can help us move from sensation, thought and feeling into KNOWING.

Perception is distinctly individual. Each of us perceives things in a unique way, influenced by our personal experiences, social conditioning, belief systems and expectations. What one person sees is often quite different from what another sees, as is evident when eyewitnesses describe what happened at the scene of an accident. As we change, so do our perceptions.

One way to broaden your perception is to read about or listen to the experiences of others. Through acknowledging their accounts, you will come to believe that such experiences are possible for you as well. Begin now to drop restrictive assumptions of what is possible. Use these affirmations to change narrow preconceptions:

If any other human being has done it, I can do it, too.

All that is humanly perceptable is perceptable to me.

Affirm that your own perceptions are widening, broadening, increasing. Your sensory powers are becoming more potent. Whatever you can imagine and believe can be true for you.

Changing Your Perception

The relationship between past and present awareness might be compared with links in a chain. To become familiar with what your past has created for you, begin to pay attention to what you are aware and unaware of now. What attracts your attention and what do you rarely notice? Do you notice people whispering in a movie theatre? Do you remember what your secretary wore today or what you had for lunch yesterday?

If you feel you have missed opportunities—not met the kind of friends you want, or not found the right job—it could be that your past intentions are controlling your present awareness. In the past, you have established what you want your inner self to draw your attention to. You have conveyed to your consciousness what things you consider important and it attracts your awareness only to these things. It allows you to ignore whatever you have decided is unimportant or uninteresting.

When your attention is drawn to something, begin to explore why. Is it a threat or an opportunity? Discover the reason for your perception. It is important to recognize the power your consciousness has to focus your awareness on whatever it wants you to see.

The following perception exercises can help you develop your powers of perception. Through expanding your perception and interests, you gain access to other realities, heighten your multisensory abilities, and sharpen your awareness so that you become more effective in your creative visualizations.

Perception exercise #1: Share an experience with a friend—go shopping, have lunch in a restaurant, take a drive, sit in a park. Afterwards, make separate lists describing your surroundings. Was anything missing that should have been there? What were the first things you noticed? Include people, sounds, smells, buildings, anything you recall. Then compare lists. This experiment reveals how each individual's reality differs greatly from another's—according to their interests.

Exercise #2: One night, unable to sleep, I arose and went quietly into my living room. My family was sound asleep and my home was very still. Without turning on a light, I sat down in an easy chair and stared into the darkness of the room. The first thing I noticed was that it was not completely dark; I could distinguish much of the room and its furnishings. But, instead of focusing on the objects in the room, I turned my attention to the dark air of the night.

I could see very faint, tiny sparks of light. Just a few at first, but seeing them stirred my interest and my focus became intense and sharp. As it did, the room filled with these sparks until dancing, darting glimmers of energy were everywhere. I wondered if my personal will could effect the light and to my surprise, when I willed the dancing lights to disappear, the room grew dark. When I willed them to reappear, the lights returned. When I chose to see them I could, when I chose not to I couldn't. On and off, I used my will as though I were flipping an electrical light switch.

Wilhelm Reich, physician and researcher, wrote of seeing these sparks of light which he called "orgone." Reichian therapists channel energy for healing, and their patients often experience these sparks following a session. Some patients have reported seeing these sparks in full daylight, walking down a crowded Manhattan street.

Exercise #3: An interior designer I know gave me this exercise. Select four pieces of fabric, each of a different unpatterned color. It doesn't matter which colors you choose. Spend a few moments looking at each of them, focusing your attention fully on first one piece then another. Try to really see the color, implanting its image in your memory.

Holding these four different colors in your mind, go out and find something else that is the exact same color as each of them. For instance, you may find a pencil that is the same color as your swatch of yellow fabric, a button that matches your red piece perfectly, a coffee cup that is exactly the same hue as your blue piece. Try the exercise using several different sets of colors. Try extending the period of time between studying the fabric swatches and finding the matching items, until you can remember the colors for several days without looking at them again.

This exercise not only helps sharpen your perceptual abilities, but also your discriminatory skills and your memory. It also can be useful when you're shopping; you'll know instantly whether a jacket in the store matches a pair of slacks you have at home! As you increase your powers of perception and discrimination, you'll be able to use them to see yourself and others more clearly, too.

Through the creative power of attention, visualization and imagination, cripples have learned to walk and cancer victims have cured themselves. In the Biblical story, Daniel used this power to protect himself in the lions' den.

All of us have the creative power to make what we want of ourselves and our environment. We are all artists. The world, our lives, our minds and beings are our canvases. Choice is the brush.

Note

1. Lorraine Dusky and J. J. Leedy, M.D., *How to Eat Like a Thin Person: The Dieter's Handbook of Dos and Don'ts.* (New York: Simon and Schuster, 1982).

5

Expanding Sensory Skills

Most people consider everything beyond the so-called "normal" range of the five physical senses *extrasensory*. It might be better to think of these as expanded sensory skills or fully-used sensory skills, however, for there is nothing extraordinary about them. All of us have these abilities if we choose to develop and use them.

Our sensory systems operate on the principle of radiation. Everything in the Universe radiates and these radiations or vibrations are sensed by one system or another. Our physical sensory organs perceive those things that radiate at a rather slow vibratory rate. Our etheric sensory systems pick up those radiating at a higher, faster rate.

As we discussed earlier, the etheric body is the prototype or psychic pattern for the physical form; therefore, the etheric sensory system is the pattern for the physical sensory system. It operates independently and is able to perceive even when the physical body and brain have no perceptual ability whatsoever. This etheric sensory system still functions when your physical body and brain are unconscious, due to anesthesia or injury (such as a coma). It's not unusual for individuals to wake up after an operation and tell you what went on while they were "out." This is the system, too, that wakes you from a sound sleep when it hears an unfamiliar sound that it feels might be threatening to you.

Animals and primitive peoples have highly developed etheric or secondary sensory systems. This secondary system enhances the first or physical sensory system which includes the five physical senses: sight, smell, touch, hearing and taste. Dowsers, too, rely on their secondary senses to locate substances hidden from their physical senses.

In our modern society, we no longer need to use our etheric systems to survive. Our basic needs for food, shelter, etc., can be taken care of by the physical sensory system, so most of us have allowed our secondary systems to grow dormant. A few humans, however, have retained or restored their higher sensory perception—we call them psychics.

The first step in reactivating and expanding your sensory skills is to believe they exist within you, available when you want or need them. Create a picture of this extrasensory system operating in you. This visualization will give your etheric system a nudge, stirring it from its slumber.

Precognition

Oddly enough, many of the things we think ordinary in animals are considered extraordinary in humans. Yet we believe humans to be a superior species. Actually, sensory systems in animals are developed to a much greater degree than our own. Precognition, or foreknowledge, which means knowing about something before it happens, is highly operative in animals. We've all heard of rats deserting a ship that's going to sink, for example. Animals also know in advance when an earthquake or volcano is about to occur and they leave the area. (If you're ever in a place where this happens, you should get out, too!) I remember watching cows in a field during a thunderstorm when I was young. Invariably, the cows would move from a spot just before lightning struck there.

In his fascinating book, *The Language of Silence*, J. Allen Boone tells of an incident of foreknowledge he witnessed. He had been observing a group of monkeys playing in the jungle when suddenly the whole group stopped still and turned in one direction, en masse. Then they ran away. Boone understood their keen sense of foreknowledge and decided to wait to see what would happen. Two hours later, several hunters with guns arrived at the spot where the monkeys had been. They said they were hunting monkeys and asked Boone if he'd seen any. An animal lover, Boone denied having seen the monkeys and out of curiosity asked the hunters when they'd left for their hunt. Their reply was, "Two hours ago."[1]

Psychic Touch

Earlier in this book, we discussed the subtle bodies which permeate and surround the physical body like balloons or clouds. These bodies can sense the presence of another being through what might be called "psychic touch." For example, if you touched me on the arm, my physical sense of touch would notice the contact. If you came up behind me and stood a foot or so away, my etheric subtle body would feel the contact through its expanded sense of touch.

For most people, this is the extrasensory skill that develops first. Many of you probably have experienced it already. If you've even "felt" another person's presence without physically touching or seeing that person, you've experienced psychic touch.

Psychic touch experiment: Your physical body is sensitive to touch but your subtle bodies are even more sensitive and discriminating. They vibrate at a much faster rate than the physical body does and are considerably larger so they sense a larger area.

The next time you are in a room with other people, focus on your subtle body. Imagine it as much larger than your physical body and think of it as having a "skin" similar to the surface of a balloon. Now picture it expanding to meet the subtle body of someone else in the room. You'll feel a slight tingling, a gentle impression of rubbing up against something else when the two subtle bodies meet.

If you try this with a friend, ask him/her to signal you when s/he senses your subtle body contact. Did you feel it at the same time? Continue experimenting at greater and greater distances as your subtle body sensitivity increases.

The skins of our subtle bodies are continually touching whenever we meet and interact with other people. Most of us are unaware of this, though we may at times sense another's presence or feel uncomfortable if someone stands too close to us. As our awareness of psychic touch develops, so does the frequency with which we experience it. Spiritual masters can expand their subtle bodies for miles, touching their students and loved ones at great distances. All things have subtle bodies and you can further heighten your sense of psychic touch by experimenting with house plants, trees and animals.

Super Sight

We know that a motion picture film is really a collection of still images, yet we see it as moving pictures. We don't see the gaps between the stills. This is because our physical eyes can only perceive at a specific and limited rate of about ten images per second. When images blink on and off more quickly we are not aware of their separateness, but the secondary system sees much more: it perceives between the frames. This secondary perceptual function is sometimes called subliminal sight. Its ability to perceive at a much more rapid rate has been capitalized upon by advertisers who inserted hidden images or messages in the "gaps" between the pictures seen by the physical eyes.

Animals see with "super sight." They see between the frames, which is why television doesn't interest them much. To them it doesn't seem real because they perceive a collection of separate, still images. I used to try to get my cat to watch TV ads with cats in them, but she wasn't fooled. Flies' vision flashes in and out so quickly that when they look at us, we're moving in slow motion. That's why they have no trouble getting away from us when we try to swat them.

Many people experience a shift into subliminal sight when they are in danger. Once when I was driving, a truck swerved into my lane. As it did, my sight slowed instantly. I could see every move the driver made, every change in his expression, until he turned the truck back into his own lane. When I was out of danger, my sight returned to its usual rhythm.

People who have used psychedelic drugs often report this same slowed, expanded vision. They see things in slow motion and moving objects appear to leave "trails" behind them. It seems that somehow the drugs alter the rhythm of ordinary sight so that these individuals temporarily see with subliminal sight.

A professional artist once told me of an unusual condition that I still can't explain. He was in his seventies and was losing his sight. He no longer could see details, only patches of color, light and shadow. One day he suddenly began seeing as if with a new set of eyes. He knew his physical eyes weren't responsible for the change because he could perceive detail much more clearly than ever before. With his altered perception, he could look at a woman thirty feet away and see not only the buttons on her dress, but the designs on the buttons as well.

He also began seeing lots of things other people didn't see at all. Finally he came to the conclusion that what he was seeing didn't exist in the physical world, but in some other realm that required extrasensory ability to perceive.

This was his reaction to going physically blind—a horrible fate for an artist. The development of his expanded senses resulted from a real need, his artist's need to see. Although he never was able to paint again since he couldn't see the canvas clearly, he nonetheless enjoyed himself and his special sight immensely.

Psychic Smell

Many people experience smells that aren't physical. That is, the smell can't be linked to anything in their physical environment. Sometimes the smell doesn't even have a counterpart in the physical world. If this happens to you, you know your secondary sensory system is working! You might be sitting next to a man who's smoking a pipe and all you can smell is his smoke. Then suddenly, you get a whiff of wet lilacs—out of nowhere. For three or four breaths, you enjoy the scent of the lilacs, then just as suddenly it's gone and all you can smell is the pipe smoke again. The lilacs simply disappeared. And nobody else in the room smelled them.

The mother of a woman I know always wore a certain perfume. After her mother died, this woman frequently thought she heard a knock on her door. When she opened it, she could smell her mother's perfume, but no one was ever there. The woman believed that her mother, who was no longer in the physical realm, was visiting and making herself known with her distinctive perfume.

Clairaudience

Clairaudience, or "clear-hearing," involves hearing with the subtle bodies. Some of the great composers, such as Mozart, Beethoven—who was physically deaf—and Bach, were known to hear the "music of the spheres." Some of these composers did not consciously decide to compose the notes of their creations, they seemed instead to hear the sounds in the ethers and simply wrote down what they heard.

The same phenomenon has been reported by people on their deathbeds who say they can hear the angels singing or the heavenly chorus playing. In some cases, people have heard this music during out-of-body experiences. I've also read about people being warned of danger by non-physical voices, sometimes the voices of departed loved ones. One well-known case is that of

St. Bernadette of Lourdes. This young French peasant girl heard the voice of the Virgin Mary speaking to her in a grotto, directing her to a curative spring where the sick and injured could wash themselves and be healed.

Such situations occur spontaneously, without conscious effort. I don't recommend trying to develop clairaudience, for the experience can be quite disconcerting and difficult to control. In addition, the voices or sounds that come to us in this way aren't always helpful to us. Just as there are non-physical entities who seek to aid us in our efforts here on earth, there are those whose aims are questionable and it is not always easy to determine the source of the material we receive.

You may recall reading about the murderer called Son of Sam, who claimed he heard a voice speaking to him through the body of a dog and ordering him to kill his victims. The world is full of self-proclaimed prophets who believe God is speaking through them, and mental institutes house many, many patients whose clairaudience torments them day and night. One woman I know frequently heard voices while she was at work. The voices became a serious distraction to her and it was necessary for her to learn to block these sounds so she could function normally. It's much more difficult to shut off hearing than to stop seeing, for instance, and opening your psychic ears may be like opening Pandora's box.

Expanding Your Secondary System

Too often we consider our inner or natural selves as inferior—just as we consider animals inferior to us. Before you can begin to expand your sensory abilities, this denigratory attitude must be dropped, for the second sensory system is the province of the natural self. Animals are in tune with their natural selves and thus have sensory systems that are much more highly developed than those of humans.

Once you have acknowledged the existence of your second sensory system, you'll want to create the will or intention to expand your sensory perceptions. Picture this system operating in you. Imagine your subtle bodies extending beyond your physical one, like concentric bubbles becoming larger and larger, finer and finer.

In his work with animals, Boone (whom I mentioned above) noticed that when he first met with a monkey, the monkey would sit very still and focus its entire attention on him. He called this practice "orienting." He learned that whenever monkeys (and other animals) did this, they were examining him to find out what they needed to know about him. Did he like monkeys? Hate them? Fear them? The monkeys looked at Boone's interior, his emotions and thoughts, not his outer appearance.

Orienting technique: You can do the same thing. Try this technique with a friend. Ask your friend to remember and re-experience a particular emotional condition, such as fear, anger, sadness, joy or excitement. Sit very still and focus on your friend's emotional state—completely. Don't let your attention wander or get distracted by outward expressions, gestures or physical features. Put your thoughts on hold and allow yourself to "feel" your friend's condition. The first emotion you experience is usually right, so don't "second guess" yourself. Now tell your friend what you believe s/he was feeling. Switch roles and let your friend orient to you. Keep score so you can see how often you're correct; chances are you'll be far above the "law of averages."

The secondary system responds to need. If your sensory abilities are a little sluggish from lack of use, you may have to create a need for them to get up and get going. Perhaps you'll have to convince yourself that developing and expanding your sensory system is important and necessary before you can get it to work for you.

One of my students wanted to be able to move objects by focusing his attention on them, but he was intimidated by other students in the class who felt his ambition was pointless. What purpose did moving pencils around on a table top serve? Because he felt his skill was unimportant, he began to doubt himself. The answer to his problem was to create a need. I convinced him that most people in our culture won't believe in extrasensory skills unless they're shown physical "proof." I told him that he had the ability to show people his skill and encourage them to believe. Soon he not only began moving things, he even made them disappear.

Interrupters

Anything that blocks the flow of radiation is an interrupter. As we discussed earlier in this chapter, everything in the Universe radiates with an energy vibration that is specific to its character or form. You've probably heard of placing an iron horseshoe above the door to keep evil spirits away. This is because magnetized iron is an interrupter. So are the branches of the rowan tree, and some cultures hang them over their doorways.

Aluminum foil, for example, interrupts noxious rays. A few years ago I met a woman who had dowsed her bedroom for noxious rays and discovered that her bed was positioned right over a ray that probably was responsible for her arthritis. Space limitations made it impossible for her to place the bed elsewhere, so she decided to put aluminum foil under her mattress. It worked! Her arthritis improved, but after a month or so, she began to suffer from arthritic pain again. It turned out that the aluminum foil had shifted and bunched up at one side of the bed, leaving her exposed to the noxious rays again.

One of the most common and powerful interrupters is thinking. Holding a belief, assumption or preconception firmly in your mind, as though it were an absolute certainty, interrupts the functioning of your second sensory system. For instance, if you believe you can't do something, you can't. Most people can't see auras or orgone--because they believe they can't.

I once witnessed a hypnotist tell his subject that when she came out of the hypnotized state, she wouldn't be able to see another person in the room, named John. It was true. When she came to, she couldn't see John. However, John was holding behind his back a rose that no one else in the room could see. The woman who had been hypnotized said, "Oh, look at that rose floating in the air!" Her belief interrupted her ability to see what she'd been told not to see, but her secondary sensory system had been altered so that she now could see what others could not.

Another example of this condition is mentioned in Magellan's diaries. Natives who had never seen sailing ships and were not conditioned to believe in such things, could not see his ships.

Early in our lives, we are conditioned to see or not to see. We are encouraged to pay attention to some things, which others consider important, and not to notice others. Many children have "imaginary friends" whom adults can't see because they have been conditioned *not* to see them. Lots of Irish people believe in the "little people" even though outsiders rarely witness these beings.

As children, we are told to hear our caretakers' words, not their tone of voice and to see their smiles, not the look in their eyes. Children who grow up with an alcoholic parent, for example, often are taught not to see the situation and even as adults may continue to deny the parent's alcoholism.

It's hard to stop thinking and just be, as most of us have discovered. Thinking interrupts sleep, meditation and lots of other things. One of my biggest problems used to be thinking while others were talking. I'd be so busy thinking about what I was going to say next, how I'd answer them, or argue with them, that I didn't really hear what they said. I was thinking so hard I missed the intonation of the voice, the emotions behind the words. My thinking was an interrupter to receiving other people's knowledge.

One evening, a friend and I were attending a lecture and I noticed my friend wasn't enjoying it. When I asked her why, she said she couldn't really focus on what the speaker was saying because he sounded like Ted Kennedy and her "inner thinker" kept interrupting her. Perhaps my friend was threatened in some way by what the lecturer was saying so her inner interrupter was keeping her from hearing him.

When our internal interrupters block our perceptions in this way, they mean well; they are trying to protect us from something they believe will hurt us. Sometimes they're protecting us from the harsh realities of life, sometimes from growth that might be difficult and painful. These interrupters are not new, active, creative processes, they're old ones that keep coming up to our awareness, rooted in outworn beliefs and structures that now are holding us back rather than helping us.

The secondary system perceives in a broader, more comprehensive manner than the physical sensory system does. For instance, have you ever been listening to someone and become uncomfortable without knowing why? This happens when the secondary system senses a change of some kind, perhaps in the tone of the person's voice, the inflection or his/her body language.

Silencing the inner interrupter: First you must accept that you are not your physical sensory system and you are not "the thinker." I must disagree with the statement, "I think, therefore I am." Words and thinking are left brain activities and they block communication from the right brain. If you have trouble meditating, as I did, you may want to try to control the thinker who keeps disturbing you.

I began with the premise that I was *not* the thinker and that I could control that part whenever I wanted. I simply commanded myself to stop thinking. Inside me, some part said "What?" Then suddenly, I was in an empty, silent canyon. I realized that the thinker in me had grown used to doing as it pleased and had become domineering. All that was necessary was for the rest of me to take charge, to stand up and demand equal time. Later, when I'd notice I was talking to myself—or rather, my self was talking to me—I'd say "shut up." And it would.

In order to expand our sensory skills to their full capacity, we first must connect with the outer world and the Universal Consciousness that is the life force of our world. According to Dr. Alexander Lowen, a healthy individual "perceives the contact between his core and the outer world. Impulses from his pulsating core (heart) flow into the world, and events in the external world reach and touch his heart . . . he feels one with the world and with the cosmos."[2]

When we block these sensory and feeling connections with other forms of life, becoming "armored" as Dr. Wilhelm Reich called it, we cannot experience or use our sensory abilities completely. As we expand our consciousness, however, we discover that we also develop "brighter vision, more acute hearing, keener smell, better taste—in other words, a higher degree of perceptual sens-ibility."[3] In short, we can enjoy ourselves and the world in which we live more if we expand our sensory skills, and we can begin to expand them by choosing to do so.

Notes

1. J. Allen Boone, *The Language of Silence* (New York: Harper & Row Publishers, Inc., 1970).
2. Alexander Lowen, M.D., *Bioenergetics* (New York: Penguin Books, 1976), p. 309.
3. Ibid., p. 312.

6

Sleep and Dreams

Every night we experience the state of sleep with scarcely a thought about its significance in our lives. Many of us take for granted those hours of slumber that separate us from the waking world, but what lessons are there to be learned in our sleep? Is there a relationship between sleep and awareness? What do our dreams really mean?

All living things have cycles of sleeping and waking. Plants and animals as well as humans rest for some portion of every twenty-four hour period. Some creatures are nocturnal—they sleep in the day and are active at night—while others are diurnal. This natural pattern of sleeping and waking, controlled by an inner body timing, is called a *circadian rhythm*. Sometimes we sleep lightly, sometimes deeply, and all of us have dreaming periods whether we remember our dreams or not. Dreaming can be detected in sleep laboratories by rapid eye movements, called REMs.

Sleep deprivation and dream deprivation affect our physical, emotional and mental health and both have been used in the past as a form of torture, mind control and punishment. Sleep deprivation can cause hallucinations, visions and altered states of consciousness, and was a common practice of solitary mystics and monks in the first few hundred years after the death of Christ. Some fanatic religious groups today use this method to create and manipulate converts. When used in conjunction with other mind control techniques, sleep deprivation can result in the destruction of personality and individuality, and a restructuring of character.

People who take tranquilizers or sleeping pills actually may be interfering with their dream cycles, causing dream deprivation. Other drugs, too, such as barbiturates, amphetamines and alcohol, can cause this phenomena.

Have A Good Night

Why do so many people have difficulty going to sleep or staying asleep? Your sub-conscious or inner self is a mirror of your attitudes, beliefs and feelings and so it reflects your deepest as well as your slightest fears and concerns. These are the gremlins, the monsters which disturb sleep. Sleep problems are not really caused by the worries of the outside world, they originate within us. Fears and anxieties indicate a distrust of the inner self, and if you distrust your inner self, your inner self grows to distrust you. If your sub-conscious self perceives itself as weak, vulnerable and dependent on the conscious self for its safety, it may be reluctant to allow you to go into a deep sleep, leaving it alone in charge of the physical body. You experience a half-sleep, a shallow rest, and wake up as tired as you were when you went to bed!

During the Middle Ages, it was commonly believed that the Devil came out and moved about at night. Sleeping people were considered most vulnerable to satanic attack. To protect themselves and others from Satan's influence, certain individuals kept watch during the night. This watch was called a *vigil*, and keeping a vigil is still a part of some religious customs. *Vigilantes* were people who pursued evil, and remaining *vigilant* meant staying awake and alert to potential danger. Many of us today are so vigilant that we allow ourselves only the most shallow sleep, afraid to drift deeper into the unknown recesses of truly restful slumber. Such vigilance prevents the separation of the astral and physical bodies, and makes dreaming impossible.

During sleep, the subconsciousness or inner self is in charge. Alert and perceptive, it relies on the sense of hearing—which becomes quite acute during periods of slumber—to provide it with information. Nighttime noises are monitored by it. All usual sounds—a dog barking, the buzz of traffic—are registered as familiar. But unfamiliar sounds, such as the crash of an automobile, are classified as unusual by the inner self; it then wakes you to investigate and take action. This is why you may experience difficulty sleeping in a strange or unfamiliar environment: the subconscious alerts you to everything unfamiliar to it.

How can you benefit most from your sleep? Anxiety and fear prevent the separation of the inner and conscious selves that must occur for a truly regenerative sleep. A regular regimen of meditation is helpful since each time you meditate, you learn to relax, to let go and achieve tranquility. You are thereby setting an example for your inner self. Your attitude toward sleep, too, can improve it—learn to anticipate sleep with delight and joy.

Review your own sleep preparation ritual. Write down the steps that you repeat each night. Are they successful for you or do you sabotage your own ritual by thinking, "I'll never get to sleep tonight?" Remember that such thoughts program your inner self, whose goal is to carry out your intention. Your inner self controls your physical body and can just as easily be directed to provide you with restful, rejuvenating sleep—if you do not oppose yourself.

Although a complete sleep cycle each night is essential for good health, many people suffer from sleep disorders. One aid is the amino acid tryptophan, available in supplement form, which helps slow brain activity and encourage sleep. Hot milk with a bit of butter is an age-old remedy to quiet the nerves and help you sleep easier. Norman Ford's book *Good Night* provides other helpful suggestions for improving sleep.

Relaxation technique "The cat": Stand up and close your eyes. In your mind, picture a cat who is about to take a nap. As you visualize it stretching, imitate the cat's movements with your arms and legs. Stretch your arms out as far as you can—stretch hard. Stretch your hands and fingers as wide as you can, then let go. Next, sit and stretch out your legs and feet. Wriggle your toes. Now relax them. Wiggle your shoulders and twist your torso, loosening tense muscles. Pretend you are a cat, *feel* like a cat who is able to let go and completely relax.

Relaxation technique #2: Lie on the floor and stretch out. Take a long, deep breath and imagine that a flow of energy is washing through your entire body. Exhale quietly, releasing your breath very slowly. Beginning with your feet, tense all the muscles and then release the tension. Repeat this with your calves, knees, thighs, abdomen, back, chest, shoulders. Feel a tingling sensation as the muscles begin to loosen. Now let your arms and hands become limp. Relax your fingers one by one. You are now totally relaxed and tranquil. As you perform this technique, you may add a visualization to relax your mind simultaneously. Imagine the cares of the day floating away, melting or dissolving.

Aligning energy patterns: Like Goldilocks, each of us has special requirements in a bed—one that is neither too soft nor too hard, but just right. The position of the bed is also an important factor. It should be placed so that the headboard faces north and the foot faces south. This lines up your physical body's axis with the planet's axis so you are in conjunction with this line of force, not lying in opposition to it.

We spend a third of our lives sleeping, so the energy that surrounds us while we sleep should be of the highest quality. During the day, we move from room to room so that the energies of any one particular space do not affect us strongly or continually. But if we are to remain still in one place for a length of time, it is wise to diagnose the energy patterns that exist there.

Dowsing is a method for finding natural energy patterns in the earth. That energy flows in the earth under your home and rises into the house. Dowsers look for what they call "noxious rays" which can cause imbalance, and ill health. You may want to contact a dowser in your vicinity to check your home, or you can learn how to dowse yourself.

Dispelling Nighttime Fears

Because our bodies are light sensitive, light triggers wakefulness—daylight or bright street lights can interfere with restful sleep. Unfortunately, for some people darkness and quiet, the very things that should improve sleep, disturb it. For those who fear darkness or quiet, nights may be an endless cycle of anxiety. The first step toward freedom from these fears is discovering their roots.

Word association exercise: One method you can use is word association. On a piece of paper list the following words: sleep, dark, light, sound, silence and awake. As you write each word, list any words that also come to mind through association. Stay with each word for at least five minutes or until you seem to have exhausted its potential. When you have completed the list, close your eyes, relax, and consider the words on the list and their associations. Explore the gestalt of these words by letting each word trigger ideas, memories or thoughts. You may gain insight into the origins of your fears, which can automatically lessen their impact.

Naming technique: If some part of you is afraid of falling asleep, give that part a nickname such as "Fearful Frank, the Scared Kid" or "Sleepless Sally."

This helps you to step outside of yourself so that you can identify what it is that's frightening you. Once you have named yourself, ask that metaphorical figure to show you who your enemy is.

Affirmations: Another way to reduce your fear of the dark or silence is to create an affirmation such as, "The dark is warm, maternal and protective, providing nurturance and rest. It feels good, is good and does good. The dark releases me from activity and stress. It is restful, calm and tranquil." An affirmation that reinforces the positive qualities of quiet might be, "Silence is powerful, permeating all without exception. Without silence there can be no sound, for sound comes from within the silence itself. I can relax in the silence, letting go all else and experience the living quality of silence itself. I can center in the silence and view all else from there. From silence, wisdom can be gained." As your inner being begins to reflect your newfound sense of safety and security in the comfort of darkness and silence, your patterns of rest and sleep will improve. When you feel secure you can let go, sleep better and awake more refreshed.

Your desire for regenerating sleep is reflected in actuality. As your intention to achieve healthful sleep becomes firm your inner self responds, providing a release from daily worries. You experience new vitality to partake of the new day.

Problem-Solving While You Sleep

Sleep tapes: Your subconscious not only monitors night sounds while you sleep, it also classifies and stores them in a memory bank. So, even while you sleep, all that is heard becomes part of your mind set—even conversations spoken during your slumber. The same phenomenon has been found to occur when you are unconscious or under anesthesia, since your inner self never sleeps and is always perceiving.

Many people use tape-recorded messages to reprogram themselves by sending subliminal messages to their subconscious selves while they sleep. Tape recordings to promote weight loss or improve self-esteem are available commercially, or you can create your own recording with a personalized programming message.

Worry dolls: These tiny South American string dolls help program your inner self to relieve your troubles. Six of them (three men and three women), each about half an inch tall, come in a minature oval wooden box. You can purchase them in some novelty shops, imported crafts stores and metaphysical shops. Or you can make them yourself.

Before going to sleep, take the dolls out of their box and hold them in your hand. You may assign each one a different problem or give all six the same problem to work on during the night. Simply explain your problem(s) to the dolls and ask them to work to find solutions while you sleep. Leave them out on your bedside table overnight. In the morning, thank them for their efforts and put them back in their box so they can rest during the day. You'll be amazed at how effective this technique is.

Technique for waking up: It is just as important to make a smooth transition from sleep to wakefulness. As you begin to wake, turn (if necessary) so your are lying on you back, keeping your eyes closed. Make sure no clothing or bedding hampers your movements. Stretch your legs loosely apart. Next, stretch your arms and legs. As you breathe in deeply through your nose, raise your arms over your head. Hold your breath and stretch from head to toe, tensing all muscles. Release the tension and exhale slowly through your nose as you drop your arms. Let your imagination roam as you lie at ease for a moment.

Dreams

Dreaming is a universal experience. It is also an intensely personal experience since no two people dream alike. Many cultures throughout history have been facinated by dreams. The ancient Egyptians erected sleeping temples for the purpose of finding answers to problems and for healing through dreams. Members the Senoi tribe center their daily lives around dream-inspired activities. Early peoples believed "the little man inside" left during sleep and returned prior to wakefulness. In Fiji, a sleeping person is never awakened for fear the wandering soul may not reunite with the body. In Burma, waking a sleeping individual is considered as discourteous as pushing him or her in the path of a truck.

Dreaming takes place at a very specific state of consciousness and usually awareness does not realize that a dream is being experienced. Whether we are aware of dreaming or not, we have four or five dreams every night. Usually, people who begin dreaming as they drift into sleep are less anxious and constricted than others who do not. Dreams that occur early in the sleep cycle are harder to recall than later ones, and introspective people recall their dreams far more readily than extroverts do.

Lucid Dreaming

As part of my research on sleep and dreaming, I decided I wanted to experience being aware during sleep. I created that intention and empowered it with determination and deep desire, asking my inner self to bring it about. On the third night after creating this intention, I slowly became aware during the night. I observed my physical body with wonder, for I had never known it to be so limp! It seemed heavy yet all of a sudden energy began to flow into my limbs. They felt as if they were swelling and becoming lighter. Then, effortlessly I slid into the waking state, without any sense of crossing a border.

I have heard similar reports from others who found themselves aware during sleep and unable to move. It is possible that this completely aware state is achieved by the separation of the physical and subtle bodies. Usually the separation and reintegration of the bodies is accomplished smoothly, but if you are shaken awake while separated, the experience can be jarring. Alarm clocks also can be jarring since they cause the physical and subtle bodies to reintegrate too suddenly. We should always wake other people gently, calling their names softly to gradually bring them to the waking state.

Lucid dreaming indicates an elevation of consciousness to a new level where aware explorations can occur in the dream state. In this state, you can control and direct your dream experiences. You also can participate in telepathic contact with another person. This is a particularly favorable place from which to do psychic healing.

If you wish, you can experience this condition, too. Simply create the intention to do so and program your inner self to achieve it for you. Tell your inner self exactly and literally what you want, knowing that it is completely capable of accomplishing the task you've given it. If you can imagine it, you can experience it. Picture what you want and why, then direct your inner self to carry out your wishes. Don't give up if you aren't successful the first, second or even third night. Just repeat your intention to your inner self, patiently and confidently.

The healthiest sleep pattern is one in which there is an actual separation of the bodies. This allows the greatest regeneration to occur. As you sink into deep states of sleep, the subtle bodies rise out of the physical body and hover about two feet above, in exactly the same shape, form and condition as the physical body. As your physical body lies prone, eyes closed, limbs flacid, an identical subtle body lies directly above, faintly luminescent. The two are connected by an *aka* cord of life energy.

Astral Projection

Occasionally, the subtle bodies rise into an upright position. Sometimes they float away from the physical body since the connecting aka cord is extremely elastic and can stretch great distances. It cannot be severed until the physical body is ready to be released in death. Many individuals have become lucid in the middle of the night and found themselves floating near the ceiling of the bedroom, looking down at their physical bodies asleep in the bed.

This experience, also called astral projection, can be frightening to some people. But others have learned to control these "out of body experiences" or OBEs and can move nearly instantaneously to any place in the Universe. They describe great adventures experienced during these astral trips.

When you dream, your body is limp, your pulse races, your eyes dart and your breathing is uneven. There is much internal action, yet, except for the eyes, little visible movement. Each night, you spend a total of about one and a half hours dreaming and, like other mammals, begin a new dream every ninety minutes. Newborns spend half of their sleeping time dreaming.

Within each of us is a dream creator, a part which devises dream sequences and creates images. Dreams have their own language—they are based in symbolism and should never be interpreted literally. Dreams provide a forum for us to unscramble our waking experiences and integrate them into our personalities. Often incomplete projects, problems or issues will resolve themselves in your dreams. Your daily experiences are reinterpreted in symbolic form so that you can learn more from them and understand yourself better. Certain themes or issues may recur in your dreams, like a serial television show that allows the characters and circumstances to develop.

Dreams are always for your benefit and the dream creator is certainly on your side. They are not something to be frightened of, since they are intended to help you. Sometimes problems you are not aware of consciously can be represented in a dream. Some individuals have even reported dreaming about physical illnesses prior to actual diagnosis.

During the day, we often are unaware of our deeper feelings, so they may surface in our dreams since the language of dreams is feelings. Dreams express how we feel about our environment, our friends, our relatives, our experiences. No dream should be dismissed as having little value for all dreams can help us understand ourselves better.

In order to learn from them, though, you need to be able to remember your dreams. Creating the intention to recall is the first step toward integrating dream teachings into your life. Since the dream creator might be divine, the intention to remember your dreams could be considered a desire to know the higher self within and to serve that self.

Keeping a Dream Journal

Show your clear intention to remember your dreams by creating a dream log or dream journal. Put this journal next to your bed on a table with a small flashlight and some pens or pencils. Since you will be writing down your dreams during the earliest moments of wakefulness, you want your dream journal to be as accessible and convenient as possible.

Some people readily remember their dreams, however, most of us do not, so it usually takes some prompting to enlist the cooperation of the inner self. Remember when programming your inner self that it accepts instructions literally. Since we have frequent dreams throughout the night, a vague intention such as "I want to recall and record my dreams" may not be clear enough. When I once used that intention I woke many times during the night, scribbled in my notebook each time, but was disappointed in the morning to find a journal full of undecipherable garble!

Start slowly, perhaps asking to remember only the last dream of the night. Specifically tell your inner self that you will wake sufficiently (but no more) to recall and write your dream down clearly. What you write is actually a short synopsis that will trigger recollection of the entire dream later. As part of your stated intention, be sure to include the desire to return to sleep until your normal waking hour. Just like a ski jumper who must learn to ski before s/he can jump, it is necessary to develop each step in the sequence of your ultimate goal.

Be sure to return to your journal entry later when you have time to focus on it and its meaning. You may want to jot down any interpretations you have of the dream. You will find your dreams usually reflect the previous day's experiences and contain your feelings about life, your environment and all the people in it.

Dream Insight and Imagery

The most helpful method of gaining insight into a dream is to recall it during a period of quiet contemplation. Think about the dream and ask yourself questions about it such as, what is the overall feeling of the dream? Happiness? Depression? Fear? Its general atmosphere is important since it is a gestalt which represents your life at this time. To gain understanding, describe the dream by beginning each sentence with, "This is my life right now...I am..."

When you dream of individuals with whom you share a relationship, the dream may be trying to convey some of your feelings about the relationship that are outside your awareness. Remember the dream is not about that person, it is about the relationship between you. Dream strangers or people with whom you have no current relationship represent some part of your own consciousness. You can understand the significance they have in your dream by placing yourself in their roles in the dream. Review the dream, experiencing it from the other person's vantage point. This technique is helpful for inanimate objects as well. Become the house, the storm, the wind, ocean or forest that is in your dream and describe yourself the way you experience it as part of that dream.

We have said that dreams work in symbolic language and sometimes the language of symbolism is quite literal. For example, since your body is the vehicle you build from birth to carry you through life, it often is symbolized as a vehicle—a car, bus or plane. Your method of symbolic transport and its condition reveals much about the state of your health and your attitudes about your body.

Your character is the aspect of yourself that you build to provide your life with structure. Therefore, it often is symbolized as a house or building in your dreams. It is important to analyze the house or building and examine its condition and contents. Is it strong, sturdy and clean? Or dilapidated and cluttered? These symbols reveal your inner character.

Water is another symbol commonly used in dream language. Water relates to your emotions and feelings. For instance, shallow water could indicate lack of feeling while deep water might convey depth of feeling. Other aspects of the water may provide further insight; is the water clear and flowing or muddy and stagnant? Fear of water can indicate reluctance to feel the emotions. A dream about swimming may symbolize an immersion into feelings.

Most children dream extensively about animals. Gradually, as they age, more and more people enter their dreams. By the time we are adults, we seldom dream about animals, but when we do the symbolism is significant. Generally, our dreams are filled with many other people, and we should work toward identifying their meanings.

Here are some other dream symbolisms that may help you to understand your dreams better.

*Horror dreams, such as chopping off someone's head, can represent unexpressed anger.

*Flying in a dream is the dream of a contented person since flying is a symbol of freedom of movement and feeling "high."

*Chase sequences in dreams suggest anxiety about a person or situation. Through free association, try to identify the source of the anxiety. Who do you feel is pressuring or chasing you?

*Paralysis in dreams indicates a feeling of impotence and helplessness. Ask yourself why you feel stuck in a rut. What aspect of your life is dull, unmoving, unchanging and lacking novelty? What's holding you back?

*Death dreams are very common and usually frightening since most of us don't realize that dreams are never literal. And because we've all heard about prophetic dreams, we assume death dreams predict an actual death. Rather, dreams about death and dying signify change and transformation. They imply that something is ending in order to make room for something new. For example, a friend of mine dreamt that her mother died and she understood that this signaled a transformation of the mother-daughter role into a new relationship between two adult women.

*Dreams about falling relate to fears of failure. In this instance, your inner self is engaging in one of its favorite creations, a pun. Falling is a metaphor for failing, i.e., "falling down on the job."

*If you find yourself alone in many of your dreams with no other living creatures participating in the dream action, it may indicate that you are quite isolated in your waking life. Being alone often signifies problems in relating to others, in allowing other people into your world or your confidence. When we feel alienated in our daily lives we may find ourselves lonely in our dream lives, wandering across empty landscapes.

*Prophetic dreams (dreams that predict the future) are not dreams in the true sense if they appear as a literal vision. Dreams always speak to us in metaphors or symbols. If, while sleeping, you witness something that later occurs pretty much the way you saw it, you actually experienced foreknowledge, astral projection or some other form of prophecy. Dreams that predict future events will do so using their usual metaphoric language.

*When you dream about another person, it is important to recognize that the dream is not really about that individual but about the relationship between you. To understand this better, you may want to give names to the people who appear in your dreams according to the roles they play for you—friend, sister, father, hero, scapegoat, confidante, therapist—in your waking life.

Interpreting dreams can be both challenging and rewarding. A positive attitude toward your dream life is recognized by your inner dream creator and will be rewarded. Your dream creator will continue to cooperate as you work toward knowledge of this side of your life. The strength of this relationship has the power to contribute greatly to your growth and fulfillment.

7

Healing

Psychic healing is often thought of as some mystical process which magically cures debilitating, even terminal illnesses in the wink of an eye. Images of faith healers, witch doctors, medicine men, voodoo priests and Brazilian psychic surgeons come to mind. But psychic healing is much broader—and simpler—than most people realize.

"Psychic healing" originates in the mind or psyche, even though its results may manifest in the physical body.

A psychic healer begins by creating a mental intention to heal, then empowers the intent with emotion and mentally projects this energy to the injured or diseased area. You can perform psychic healing on yourself or on another individual, animal or plant.

Healing is a process of transformation, of changing the body from a state that is out of balance or ill into one that is whole and healthy. Good health involves constant change and movement forward in evolution. In the words of Cardinal Newman, "To live is to change, and to be perfect is to have changed often."[1] The continual pursuit of self-fulfillment and self-actualizaiton keeps us in optimal health. Fear blocks forward movement and life energy stagnates, then subsides.

The Subtle Bodies

Each of us actually has many bodies. Disorders or sickness in any one of them may show up in the others as well. Because all are closely interrelated and dependent on each other, often it is necessary to heal on several different levels before total health is restored.

The etheric and the physical bodies are so closely connected they act almost as one unit. Because of the strong bond between the two, curing one often will affect a cure of the other. The *etheric body*, is the "negative" body; the physical or *sensation body* is the "positive" body. The physical body acts as a vehicle for experiencing the physical world. The etheric body might be thought of as a body mold, a pattern for the physical body's ideal state. It cannot be harmed by physical effects, and is without emotion, feeling or sensation. However, it can be filled with feeling by the *astral body*, which injects feeling into it through vortices known as the chakras.

A strong, healthy etheric body fills the physical body with an abundance of energy and the physical form flourishes with the life force delivered to it. This life force, also called chi, prana, orgone and many other names, flows through meridians that parallel the nervous system. By directing the flow of energy through these meridians, acupuncturists, polarity therapists, reflexologists and other healers are able to correct imbalances that contribute to disease.

The etheric body is flexible, able to contract and expand. When it is healthy and secure, the etheric body is fully expanded into the flesh and provides the physical body with all the vital energy it requires.

The etheric body responds to the sensations of the physical body instantly. But sometimes the physical body's experiences actually originate in the etheric body. For example, your feet or hands grow cold when the etheric body contracts and withdraws its life energy from those extremities.

The *astral body* is connected to the limbic or "feeling" brain. Therefore, this body is particularly susceptible to disharmony of feelings. It recognizes that the most important part of living is *feeling* alive. Also known as the emotional body, the astral body is gaseous, a virtual cloud of energy. Together with the etheric body, it makes up a vehicle in which the spirit (or soul, entity, monad) lives, moves and experiences thinking and feeling.

The astral body vibrates at such a rapid rate that it normally cannot be seen. However, we have the potential to develop "astral sight" and see each others' astral bodies, just as our physical eyes see our physical bodies.

The Chakras

Each subtle body has a boundary which is equivalent to the skin of the physical body. This boundary serves as an interface between the body and the outside world. In that interface are vortices (like the pores in our skin) that absorb and discharge many kinds of energies. These subtle body openings are known by the Sanskrit word *chakras*. There are seven major chakras for "breathing" in energies. The first, or root chakra, is located at the base of the spine and draws in earth energies. The second chakra, positioned a bit higher in the body, draws in elemental water or "liquid energy" known as *prana* or *mana*. The third chakra, centered in the area of the solar plexus, breathes in electrical or fire energy. The fourth chakra, near the heart, draws in subtle air energy. The force entering at the heart chakra is associated with the capacity to feel. The force moving in at the fifth chakra, which is located in the throat, influences the capacity to communicate. The sixth chakra, found at the brow, is involved with greater sensory perception, and the seventh, or crown chakra, with higher understanding and wisdom. There are many other smaller chakras or vortices in each body boundary, but through understanding the functions of the major ones we can begin to comprehend the vortex principle.

In most of us, some of our chakras are large and powerful, others weak and small. Their condition reflects the many choices we have made throughout our lives. As our choices change, so do our chakras. When we are willing to let these forces enter and work within our personalities, the respective chakras will enlarge and bring them in for us.

The first chakra's principle issue is security. If you feel your security lies "out there" this chakra will be underdeveloped. Feelings of insecurity and inadequacy—particularly of a sexual nature—affect this chakra, as do stress, anxiety and hatred.

The second chakra is a source of sensuality and sexuality. It can be a source of high energy and vitality when you are willing to develop strong sexual relationships.

The third chakra is your center of power, self-confidence and assertiveness. Its fire power gives you the energy to fight if you must, converting fear to courage. Related to the sun, this chakra also is associated with ambition.

The fourth chakra brings in the power to feel, to respond deeply from the heart, to love others. By opening this chakra you develop compassion, empathy and the power to heal the emotional pain of others. Through it comes the ability to feel truly alive.

The fifth chakra draws in creative power, the power to express your will. This force can increase insight and understanding. It also is the source of your sense of authority and responsibility, and your ability to make decisions.

The sixth chakra is sometimes called the third eye. This force helps you become aware of who you are, have been and can be. You can use this energy center to help overcome difficulties and get in touch with divine forces and your own spiritual nature. This force also can heighten your subtle or "extra" sensory abilities.

Seventh chakra forces can help you overcome apathy, complacency and cynicism. Through this door pass highest wisdom, the power to gain mastery over all your selves and recognition of the "rightness" inherent in the Universe. The highest intuitional capacity resides here.

Chakra exercise: You can focus attention on any one of the chakras with the intention of increasing its participation in your life. As your attention rests on its target, the chakra will respond. Relax, breathe deeply and become tranquil before you begin. Sit quietly, eyes closed, and focus a beam of mental energy on the part of your body where the particular chakra resides. After a moment, you will feel a tingling in that chakra. You can enhance the effects of this exercise by directing a visualization of color to the chakra. (See chapter 4 for more information about using color.)

Attitude and Health

By now, even conservative medical practitioners agree that attitude influences health. Persons with strong "wills to live" may survive when all odds are against them, and it isn't uncommon for others who believe they have nothing to live for to die without appearing truly ill. Our reactions to stress may increase blood pressure, cause ulcers or bring on a stroke. Depression leaves us feeling devitalized so we may succumb to colds, flus or worse. Conversely, when we are happy and enjoying life we rarely experience disease. The word "dis-ease" actually indicates imbalance and disharmony, being out-of-sync with life's rhythms. When we work against the natural rhythms in our lives our bodies are not nurtured and restored; instead they are worn down.

Wilhelm Reich, a controversial psychiatrist and physician who worked in Europe and the United States during the first half of this century, linked cancer to depression, lack of aggression, and an attitude of giving up which he called "characterological resignation."[2]

Arnold Hutschnecker, author of *The Will to Live*, believes that people who feel bound by obligations from which they want to be free are candidates for sudden, serious illness.[3] Perhaps the best-known proponent of the belief that attitude can bring on disease or facilitate recovery is Norman Cousins. According to Cousins, "Panic is a killer...(it) can destabilize the heart and sometimes even rupture heart muscles."[4] When he, himself, suffered two coronaries, he chose laughter as his medicine. By enjoying comic tales and humorous movies and TV shows, he succeeded in laughing himself well—not once, but twice![5]

Self-image has a lot to do with the health of the physical, emotional and feeling bodies. For total health, acceptance, love and caring must be present. We must accept, love and care for all our bodies and see them as being equally important. An attitude that one is superior to another can corrupt the relationship between them and have a deleterious effect on all.

The same attitude may manifest differently in each body, however, according to the nature of that body's functioning. Longing for the past, for example, may bring "craziness" in various forms since craziness means unclear thinking, the opposite of clarity. In the astral body, longing for the past may bring psychosis, in the etheric body, neurosis. In the physical body, you may find evidence of cancer, a physical expression of cells "gone crazy."

On occasion, we may suffer from health problems that originate in someone else. This *sympathetic response* to another's illness is most evident in babies who often are affected by the moods or physical conditions of their mothers. As adults, we may suffer from headaches, stomach pains or emotional upsets when someone close to us is experiencing some type of distress.

But, overall, your health is a direct result of your intentions. You have the power to create healthy conditions for yourself and others. By working within the structure of natural law, you can manifest health in all aspects of your life. Illness, disease or accident is not the result of fate but of the quality of life you experience. Intellect, imagination, intuition, attention and intention are the building blocks of good health and the basis for performing the techniques described in this chapter.

Healing Yourself

Healing with Color

In chapter 4, we looked at some of the properties of color and ways color may be used to improve our psychic, emotional and physical well-being. Color can be an important part of psychic healing. You can focus visualizations of the appropriate color on a specific, ailing part of the body, or imagine yourself surrounded in a cloud of one or more colors as needed. You also can use the same technique to aid another's healing process by focusing mental beams of color on him/her. Or, you can purchase an incandescent light bulb of the necessary color and sit under it, letting the colored light envelop you.

The following list shows which colors aid which conditions, however, you may want to refer back to chapter 4 for more information.

Red—vitalizes, energizes, stimulates; provides assertive, masculine or yang energy for the physical body and the emotions.

Orange—similar to red, but more balanced, less agitating.

Yellow—balances the nervous system.

Green—for healing physical injuries; promotes growth of new tissues.

Blue—for infections, sterilizes and relieves inflammation; calms and tranquilizes, reduces over-stimulation or excitement.

Purple/Violet—increases self-esteem.

Pink—calms emotional tensions, fears and disturbances; promotes self-love and elevates self-esteem.

White/Clear—strengthens the immune system; acts as a psychic bandage to protect against injury or infection, can be "wrapped" around an area that has been treated with another color to seal in the healing energy.

Gold—increases "masculine" mental activity (intellect, rational thinking); balances an overly emotional condition; balances the nervous system.

Silver—increases "feminine" mental activity (intuition, emotion); balances an overly intellectual condition; heightens intuition.

Color also can be used as a diagnostic tool. In 1947, Swiss psychologist Max Lüscher introduced his Color Test at an international medical conference in Lausanne. A subject taking this test selects and arranges colors in order of preference. The results reveal a wealth of information about the individual's psychological dynamics, emotional state, glandular condition and level of stress. A shortened version of the test was published in his book *The Lüscher Color Test*.[6]

Fantasy game "Colored rays": Find a time and place when you will be undisturbed. Arrange beforehand to have a friend read the following script or pre-record it yourself on tape. Wear loose clothing and sit in a comfortable chair while you listen to this script.

Close your eyes, relax and get comfortable. Let all tension and stress float away, let the cares of the day lift from your shoulders. Now, see yourself walking in a pine forest. It is a warm summer day and you're walking barefoot. You can feel the soft pine needles like a cushion under your feet. Soon you come to a circle of pine trees. You enter the circle and feel the golden radiance of the sun falling all around you.

Stand there for a few moments, then silently invoke the Golden Ray Vibration. See this beam of golden light surround you and fill your body. Ask it to heal you in the way that is most appropriate for you, and visualize yourself merging with the light, becoming one with the Golden Ray Vibration. Now ask whether it has anything to teach you and allow yourself to be in total harmony with this vibration, receptive to its teaching.

Let the Golden Ray fade away and bring in the Red Ray to surround you and permeate all your bodies. Feel this color flowing through your blood stream, giving you new vitality and confidence. Red energizes and revitalizes you. See this red as a translucent, vibrant, rich ruby red color. After basking in it for a few moments, let the Red Ray change to the deep Rose-Pink Ray. Visualize this color surrounding and permeating all your bodies. Feel yourself becoming one with this color of universal love which brings you renewed youthfulness and joy. Let the Rose-Pink Ray heal any sorrow you have and restore you to optimum health.

Next, invoke the radiance of the Orange Ray Vibration. See it revitalize your glandular system as it balances and grounds you. Feel yourself filled with optimism and cheer, buoyed by the energy of the Orange Ray.

Now, invoke the Yellow Ray Vibration and let it surround and permeate you. Feel it softening old resistances and dispelling fears. You can feel your outlook on life becoming more positive. Translucent, shimmering yellow nourishes your nervous system and strengthens your cognitive powers.

Once again, become aware of being in the center of the circle of pine tress. Notice that the Green Ray Vibration is streaming toward you from the trees. Be at peace and harmony with the Green Ray as it surrounds and imbues your whole being. Let it restore your balance and bring you harmony and serenity. Feel it trigger within you a power to grow and unfold your potential.

Now, let the Blue Ray from the sky surround and fill all your bodies. Feel its soothing, calming effect. All your tension disappears as the Blue Ray penetrates and heals you, enveloping you in tranquility.

Indigo, the color of the velvety night sky, now appears and blesses you. It carries with it the vibration of feminine power. Bathe in this Indigo Ray and experience the mother aspect of your own high self that cares for and protects you.

As the Indigo Ray fades, a vibrant Violet Ray surrounds you. Purple (or violet) has the transformative power to heal by destroying all disharmony, conflict and discord in your bodies. It removes all limitations and restrictions that have blocked your natural expression. Let it wash you clean of all false belief and misunderstanding.

Now, ask the Silver Ray to be with you and feel it surround you. It enters you and brings with it the life energy to transform your consciousness. Feel its gleam of silver light elevate you to new heights of vision and experience.

You feel lighter and lighter as the Silver Ray changes into brilliant White Light. Feel yourself becoming one with the White Light, feel total love, total health, total happiness and joy. Feel the security of being surrounded by this Divine Presence that fills the Universe.

Sit quietly and let these experiences be absorbed into your consciousness. Thank your inner self for its aid in bringing this experience to you. Now open your eyes, stretch as if waking from a deep sleep, and resume your daily activities feeling renewed, refreshed and healed.

Healing with Sound

Some people think of music as therapy for the soul, but I believe sound also can be a prescription for physical health. We are surrounded by all sorts of sounds—birds chirping, traffic buzzing, bells ringing, machines clanking, and many others that are inaudible to the human ear. These sounds vibrate at varying rates and the different vibrations produce different tones.

Harmony is equated with well-being, disharmony with dis-ease. The structure of body harmonics, once understood, can be used to reinforce health. As discussed earlier, we are comprised of different bodies, and each body has seven chords of notes which correspond with the seven chakras. Consequently, it is possible to "tune" your body by playing the notes which harmonize with it.

An octave is a unit of musical measurement and contains seven notes: A, B, C, D, E, F and G. The lower octaves resonate in your physical body. The next seven notes resonate within your etheric body, the next octave in your astral body, the next higher octave in the mental body and the highest in the spiritual body. By playing and listening to these notes, you can help bring your bodies into harmony with one another, thereby increasing your vitality, balance and health.

Another way to "tone" the body is to listen to music you enjoy. As you do so, create the intention that your body will respond to whatever tones you need to restore harmony in your bodies. Visualize your bodies uniting in perfect health. If you wish, you may use different music for each body.

New Age music: Music can soothe the savage beast in each of us. But too much of the music we hear every day is destructive, deadening, causing dissonance within our bodies and aggression and hostility in our environments. New Age music strives to create a counterpoint to these harmful sounds and rhythms. It recognizes a deeper meaning in sound and rhythm, realizing that music affects our minds, our moods and our spirits.

New Age musicians compose music specifically designed for meditation, to deepen concentration and to enhance creativity. Some New Age music also has the power to heal the physical body and transform emotional conditions.

Many healing centers now accept the relaxation properties of certain kinds of music and use it as part of therapy.

Because our bodies—all our bodies—resonate to the sounds in our environments, we are adversely affected by noxious, agitating, injurious sounds, even when we consciously tune them out. Often the result is stress. New Age music offers a balm to all this auditory irritation. By using carefully orchestrated rhythms, tones and vibrations, it encourages feeling expression and communion with higher consciousnesses. It expands perception and insight and seeks to fill the background of our lives with harmony and serenity.

New England Sound Healers, a group of musicians and healers in Lexington, Massachusetts, produces music to use in conjunction with quartz crystals. The music of Jonathan Lyghte and Michael Noll (known as Spirit

Sounds) may be used for meditation, healing, relaxation and a "variety of interdimensional experiences." The rhythm of their music is believed to attune brainwaves to an alpha state. It also causes the chakras to resonate, balancing energy patterns in the physical and subtle bodies. They use the keynotes of F (the fundamental tone of the earth, according to the ancient Chinese) and C (believed to be the harmonic of the Ionosphere) to help center the listener with the Universe.[7]

When we listen to New Age music we are trying to tune in and resonate to the "angelic chorus." Classical composers, whose music has endured for centuries, also heard the "music of the spheres" through their higher sensory organs. Plants have been found to respond most favorably to classical music, which nurtures them and promotes their healthy growth. People who are near death often mention hearing angels singing to welcome them into the next dimension.

New Age music is concerned with the lyrics in songs as well as the rhythms and tones, since words create suggestions that can become beliefs. For instance, instead of portraying love as being filled with pain and suffering, as is common in popular music, New Age songs depict a more positive vision of love.

As our awareness expands, our intelligence and discrimination increase and with them our understanding of the importance of music in our lives.

Signing

Signing is a healing technique that uses physical activity as a modality for change. We stamp our feet, for example, to release anger that, if suppressed, could jeopardize our health. There are many ways to use physical expression as a healing technique. You can "sign" self-confidence by holding your shoulders back, your head high.

Dr. Alexander Lowen designed a series of physical positions, movements and exercises called "bioenergetics" which he used in treating patients with psychological problems. Bioenergetic exercises relieve tension and help the individual experience a sense of well-being. One fundamental position called the "bow" involves arching the back so that the body resembles a drawn bow. This exercise releases stress and creates a feeling of integration, of being centered or grounded.[8]

Releasing technique #1: This is best done outdoors, but you can perform it successfully indoors if you have enough room. Stand with your feet slightly apart, your shoulders back and your head high. Each time you exhale shout "ha." Breathe as fast as you can, shouting "ha" on every outbreath. Let your voice grow louder and clearer with each breath. Feel your repressed emotions coming out as you shout "ha." Give each emotion a turn, allowing "ha" to express whatever you have been holding in. Visualize all this stagnant, frustrated energy leaving your body, making room for fresh new energy to enter.

Releasing technique #2: Sit at a table and place your hands on the table top in front of you. Pre-record the following list of emotions and the accompanying signal "now." (If you prefer, you can create your own list of emotions or add to this list.) When you hear the command "now," press down on the table top with your hands and fingers. This is fun to do with a group of friends, and sharing experiences afterward can be helpful to all.

Anger	now!	Hate	now!
Grief	now!	Love	now!
Joy	now!	Passion	now!
Reverence	now!	Devotion	now!
Caring	now!	Sadness	now!
Happiness	now!	Enthusiasm	now!
Optimism	now!	Pessimism	now!
Depression	now!	Anxiety	now!
Eagerness	now!	Resentment	now!
Hostility	now!	Impatience	now!
Irritation	now!	Exaltation	now!

This experiment can help you become aware of locked up emotions—both positive and destructive ones—and how your body responds to them. It is useful for releasing destructive feelings you have been holding back. It also can help you recognize which constructive feelings you're having trouble expressing; when those words are sounded, the pressure of your hands will lack force. Once you are aware of your feelings you can set about designing channels for their useful expression.

Joy of movement exercise: Let your entire body begin to move to the rhythm of your breathing. Jump up and down. Swing your arms. Jerk or sway. Wriggle, twist and squirm. Do whatever feels good. Feel yourself releasing all tension, anxiety and irritability, making room for playful, joyous feelings. Let your jumping and swinging become a celebration of life. Throw your arms over your head, swing your legs high to express your ecstasy at being alive. Have fun!

After you've spent about ten minutes jumping, shouting and moving about vigorously, lie on the ground or floor. Remain limp and motionless. Experience the contrast of inactivity. Center in silence, focusing your attention on silence itself. Space is silent. Silence is resounding all around us all the time. When you are totally quiet and still you actually can hear that silence. Spend about ten minutes lying quietly, enjoying this period of inactivity.

Dance your cares away: Although our nature is to respond to earth's rhythms with body movement or dance, most of us restrict our bodies' responses and decrease our sensitivity to rhythm. In so doing, we have lost not only our aptitude for dancing but our connection with the subtle rhythms of nature. This exercise will help you renew your relationship with the natural world. You can do it alone, with a friend or in a group.

Choose music with a rhythm that appeals to you. In a spot where you have room to dance, play the music you've selected and begin moving freely, expressing whatever you feel. Observe your body closely. Is it awkward or graceful? Which parts move freely and which do not? What is your body expressing? How do you feel about doing this? Keep dancing and observing the changes that occur as your body relaxes and begins to enjoy this activity. Try some different dance steps. Try whirling and spinning. Don't criticize or inhibit yourself, just let your body move freely. Dance for at least ten minutes and work up to half an hour.

Healing through Visualization

Visualization is one of the most powerful "elixirs" in the psychic healer's medical bag. In much the same way you would use visualization techiques to get a job, win a tennis match or protect yourself, you can heal yourself and others.

Dr. Carl Simonton utilized the tremendous healing capabilities of the subconscious mind (or natural, inner self) in his work with cancer patients. In his book *Getting Well Again* he tells how his patients were able to treat themselves using the power of their minds.[9] By visualizing themselves well they encouraged their inner selves to combat and destroy the cancer cells. Many hospitals and health establishments throughout the country now use Simonton's methods in their cancer treatment programs.

The same techniques can be used in curing the common cold, mending a broken bone and countless other situations. The first step is to assume responsibility for your own health and stop looking outside—to "professionals" or medications—to provide relief. Realize that *you* have the power to correct the problem and restore balance to your system. Without your will, desire and cooperation, no amount of "doctoring" will heal you.

Goal visualization technique: Use any of the relaxation methods discussed earlier to put yourself in a meditative state. In your mind's eye, create a picture of yourself in perfect health. This is your "goal," the end result you are moving toward in your visualizations. Your vision should be explicit and literal, mentally existing right now, in the present. If you want to heal a broken leg, for example, imagine the leg completely well and strong. Realize that your inner self knows the best way to heal the leg, so you don't need to direct it in the specific steps of the process. Now release the intention to your inner self with perfect confidence that it will become actualized; self-doubt can result in failure.

The Healing Wand

Remember the fairy godmother's magic wand? Now you can make your own. This rod is a powerful tool, so keep it tucked away in a safe and private place and never use it for anything but healing the physical body.

A magic healing wand can be made of any material. Some of the wands available through occult stores are quite elegant: silver or even gold, often decorated with quartz crystals or gemstones. You may choose to make yours out of something simple, however, such as a wooden rod. Remember to use natural materials, not synthetics such as plastic or alloys like aluminum.

You can pour your life force into any appropriate container, where it will be stored until you are ready to heal with it. To charge a healing wand, grasp it with both hands. Imagine the water-like energy of your life force pouring forth from your hands into the rod as you recite the following affirmation:

"I, (your name), now pour from each hand a bountiful supply of life force (or prana, chi, orgone) which flows into the object I hold. These two forces now join, creating a third force which is greater than the two. This third force has the power to heal and balance any biological dissonance or disharmony. This force field radiates outward as a loving and beneficent power. Whenever I touch the tip of this wand to any part of my body, that part will respond with love and harmony, and move into synchronized rhythm with the rest of my body."

When it is not in use, wrap your wand in a piece of soft cloth of a natural fibre, such as linen or silk. This will protect it from light and hold in your own body's frequency pattern. Use it only on your body. Do not let others handle your magic wand or even look at it since their body frequencies can interfere with its efficiency. Recharge it after each use and store it in a safe, dark place.

Affirmation for health: Your body is continually renewing itself, changing every second. In the newness of each day, you can experience freedom from former impediments to health. Make a practice of reciting the following affirmation at least once each day, preferably in the evening. By letting go of everything that might block optimum health, you give your body a chance to make itself whole and perfect.

Sit down, relax, close your eyes and repeat the following: "I now release all the day's experiences. Any unexpressed energy now flows out of me and is dissolved in the atmosphere. I relax in the process of regeneration and restoration; I now exist in balance and harmony."

Strengthening your aura: When you are relaxed and at ease, the brightness of your aura increases. As you accept well-being, your aura reflects your good health. Your aura is heavily influenced by the company you keep; some people sap its energy, making it dim and weak, while others expand and brighten its light. Become discriminating about the people with whom you spend time. Eliminate all associations that do not nourish your self-esteem and well-being. Use affirmations and visualizations to bring white light into your personal atmosphere. This will strengthen your aura and increase your resistance to destructive influences.

Healing Others

The desire to relieve another's distress is innate and sometimes our response to someone else's suffering is very strong indeed. But in our work to aid others we must use discrimination. We need to remember that our psychic and personal powers are "strong medicine" and can do more harm than good when used in an incorrect manner.

Whenever we influence other people with our personal powers we must be very careful not to manipulate or control them. We must never judge another or presume to know what is right or wrong for him/her. Each individual must be free to use his or her own will, to make decisions and to accept or reject our efforts.

The most acceptable energy we can radiate to another has the quality of "caring." If you silently repeat the phrase, "I care about you," whenever you send healing energy to another person and hold an image of that person in your mind, a warm, nurturing force will move directly toward your target. Sometimes you can feel this energy leaving you and the recipient becomes aware of a warm glow as his/her life field absorbs your incoming energy. But you still must allow the other individual to decide whether to accept or reject your attention.

Healing with love energy: Begin by sending caring energy, as discussed above, toward a specific individual. (You also can do this for an animal or plant.) Follow with a visualization of bright, clear light and surround the person you wish to heal with it. If any dark areas persist in this picture, continue imagining pure white (clear) light until you can see the individual bathed completely in the light.

When you are satisfied with this image, begin sending mental patterns of good health, personal happiness, abundance, social or career success—whatever this person needs to be healthy and whole. Visualize the end product, the healing process completed, rather than the steps necessary to get there. As you send this visualization, you may wish to augment it by verbalizing a full description of the healed condition. When your objective has been accomplished, you may feel a sense of release, hear a "click" or simply *know* intuitively. Now end the healing with the words, "It is done."

Healing with symbols: Relax, get comfortable, close your eyes and move into a tranquil state where you can focus intently. You need to know the name of the person you're going to heal. A picture of that person is helpful, too. Review the problem and symptoms that are known, but allow your intuition to bring additional information to your awareness as well. As you silently speak the person's name, allow his/her image to arise in your mind. Let your inner self draw pictures for you that illustrate the subject and his/her condition. For example, you may ask your inner self to use black spots on the body image to indicate areas of concern.

When you feel you have a clear image of your patient, visualize that person lying on a treatment table. Now proceed to treat your patient using imaginary tools. Use such things as vacuum cleaners to "clean out," tape or glue to "patch up," brushes to stimulate, string to mend. When you have finished your ministrations, see your patient rise from the table and stand before you for inspection. Let your inner self examine him/her and tell you if the job is complete. If so, release the picture and let it go; if not, repeat the process and do some additional work.

You can give your inner self some symbols to work with when you use this process. A Valentine heart, for example, could stand for a physical heart, and its rosy-red color could indicate health. Thus, a pale pink heart might reveal anemia, a dark red one high blood pressure, a broken heart emotional trauma, etc. To heal a broken heart, you can open up the patient's chest (visually) and tape the pieces back together.

Blood vessels might be symbolized as plastic tubing. If you see a blockage in one of the tubes, you could use an imaginary vacuum cleaner to suck out whatever is impeding the free flow of blood to the body. A picture of a limp rag doll might symbolize lack of vitality. You could take an imaginary bicycle pump and pump energy into that doll until it stands up full of life. Use your imagination to create some interesting and efficient symbolic healing methods, and train your inner self to become proficient in using them.

Illness and injury are not unfortunate accidents. Nor are they "the will of God," the result of fate or heredity. All healing power resides in us, in our own inner selves. Our wills and beliefs determine how effective any healing can be. This is why a placebo may be just as beneficial to an ailing patient as a potent drug, why faith healers really can "cure" illnesses, why a mother's kiss soothes a child's pain. In our culture, healing such as we've discussed in this chapter might be considered "magic," though in truth there is nothing strange or magical about it. Health is our birth right, our natural state of being.

Notes

1. Celestial Seasonings, Inc., 1780 55th Street, Boulder, Colorado.
2. Wilhelm Reich, *The Cancer Biopathy* (New York: Farrar, Straus and Girous, 1973), p. x.
3. Arnold A. Hutschnecker, *The Will to Live* (New York: Cornerstone Library/Simon & Schuster, Inc., 1966).
4. Norman Cousins, *The Healing Heart: Antidotes to Panic and Weakness* (New York: W.W. Norton & Co., 1983), p. 35.
5. Norman Cousins, *Anatomy of an Illness as Perceived by the Patient: Reflections on Healing and Regeneration* (New York: W.W. Norton & Co., 1979) and *The Healing Heart: Antidotes to Panic and Weakness* (New York: W.W. Norton & Co., 1983).

6. Dr. Max Lüscher, *The Lüscher Color Test*, edited and translated by Ian Scott (New York: Pocket Books/Simon & Schuster, 1969).

7. Goldman, Jonathan S. and Noll, Michael. *Windows of Sound*. (Lexington, Mass: Spirit Music, 1984).

8. Alexander Lowen, M.D., *Bioenergetics* (New York: Penguin Books, 1976), pp. 72-74.

9. O. Carl Simonton, M.D., Stephanie Matthews-Simonton and James Creighton, *Getting Well Again: A Step-by-Step, Self-help Guide to Overcoming Cancer for Patients and their Families* (New York: Bantam Press, 1978).

8

Being and Becoming

We assume physical incarnation here on earth to learn and grow. When pursued, this purpose gives life meaning. By looking at our lives in this context, we can see how well or poorly our goals and programs are working. For when we are no longer learning and growing, when the activities we engage in no longer have meaning for us, we suffer what is commonly called "burnout." Our natural, instinctive response is to quit those activities because they have been fully explored, and to move on to something that will bring back the sense of purpose and meaning to our lives, something that will allow us to continue learning.

"In the life of the mind," says Lawrence J. Bendit, "whenever one reaches a certain goal one finds that it is not a goal but a sign-post pointing the way to a further stage of understanding."[1]

Before we assume physical form on this planet, we are part of a larger consciousness. The most forceful quality of that portion of consciousness is the urge to learn and grow, to move from ignorance into an expanded, multi-dimensional experience filled with wisdom and intelligence and to become a co-creator with the highest powers of Divine Mind. This tremendous urge moves every single being toward situations or contexts within which learning can take place. Physical incarnation is only one context in which this can happen, but it is the one we have chosen at this time. Becoming is the process of creating a wiser, more expanded being.

Because we beings have creative powers, as discussed earlier, we create personalities to go along with the physical bodies we've entered. Personality is a vehicle for the pursuit of knowledge. A personality serves many purposes, one of which is to preserve and maintain the physical body so it can continue to learn. Another is to create situations that provide opportunities for growth and development. By allowing certain material to enter the personality—from other people or of its own design—the being "programs" the personality with guidelines and directions, and those ideas, beliefs, behaviors and attitudes become part of the personality.

Programming

The concept of programming often is associated with computers. But since the beginning of time we actually have been "programmers" of the world's most sophisticated computer: the human mind. The methods by which we establish our belief systems, values, characters and personalities are the result of our programming. Just as we program a computer to respond in certain ways, we ourselves are programmed to believe, value and respond in particular ways.

Like the computer, which cannot initiate anything it is not programmed for, the inner self relies on programming by the conscious self. The inner self is the builder, the creator of all we manifest personally, but it does not design the patterns of that creation. These programs must come from its "boss," the conscious self.

Each of us is, in essence, the culmination of our programming. For example, all physical actions are accomplished by the inner self under the direction of the conscious self, but the manner in which a physical action is performed is the result of programming. The way a ball is thrown reflects the experiences and attitudes that accompanied the learning of that skill.

All of us are pre-programmed to an extent since we are born with physical aptitudes for walking, talking, gesturing, laughing and crying. Most children fulfill this programmed potential, yet each child reflects its teachers or guides in the performance of these programs. From the combination of outside influences (parents, teachers, etc.) and conscious experiences, the inner self shapes each child's character, personality, beliefs, attitudes and emotional nature.

When we become adults, we are ready to assume responsibilty for our own selves and become their primary programmers. We have the opportunity and power to change any established programs and create new ones of our own choice.

Pre-birth Programming

I believe that all of us have lived many lifetimes in various physical bodies. When we were "new souls" just starting out on this road of birth and re-birth, we didn't have much to say about the conditions of our earthly lives. Our "destinies" were chosen for us by the Powers That Be, who rule the evolutionary processes of the Universe. But as we grew in wisdom and experience, we earned the right to make some decisions about our life paths. We were able to "program" ourselves, to assign ourselves certain goals to work toward while in physical forms.

We learn through making choices and as we develop greater skills and intelligence, we are given more opportunities to choose. In any specific physical incarnation, we may or may not have the opportunity to chose such things as when and where to be born, into which sex, race, culture, level of society, family, family position, etc. One day, we will be able to choose whether or not we even want to incarnate.

At this stage, most of us here have made some choices for ourselves and have had some made for us by other, wiser beings, in order to create contexts within which we can learn. Those of us who are most skillful at making choices and who have been willing to learn much in previous lives had a larger selection of choices available to us before we took physical form this time on earth. Those of us who have resisted learning in past lives may not have been given many options. Higher Mind may have "assigned" certain conditions that will force the learning process to take place. Free choice is not exactly a God-given right. It is a privilege we earn through making the right choices. Thus, the skill to choose wisely is one we should value highly and seek to develop as fully as possible.

Perhaps you feel you came to earth to accomplish something special, to fulfill a particular destiny. Perhaps you feel you have a pre-ordained mission or life-purpose, such as serving others or bringing a "message" to the world. I don't believe such is the case, except, perhaps, for those very wise, highly-evolved souls who have total choice over their own fates.

In recent years, past-life recall has become quite popular. Many people seeking to understand their present-life circumstances better are turning to *hypersentience*, hypnosis, psychic life readings, astrology and other practices to discover something about their previous incarnations. In my earlier book, *Develop Your Psychic Skills*,[2] I mention a few techniques for delving into your past lifetimes.

Technique for discovering goals and intentions: Here is another way you can gain information about your goals here on earth and the learning experiences you've chosen for yourself in this lifetime. Look at situations in your current life that seem to be repeated again and again. Perhaps you have had a series of unsuccessful marriages and relationships. Maybe you find yourself in job after job where your talents are overlooked.

Sometimes the issue or situation repeats in a slightly different way each time. For example, if your problem is with authority figures, this may show up initially as conflicts with your parents, later with teachers, employers, police, etc. Or, if your "goal" is to learn to manage your resources, you may experience situations that require you to manage your health and vitality better (physical resources) and others where you must find ways to manage your money and property (material resources).

Repetition is a great teacher and each repetition is an opportunity. Until a necessary lesson is learned, you cannot advance in the "school of life." Until a condition is resolved, you will be continually provided with opportunities to recognize the problem area and rectify it. Lessons not learned in the past—in this lifetime or previous ones—will come up again and again, in new circumstances, in new contexts. The more pain or difficulty you experience in the problem area, the more pressing the need to do something about it. Often it seems that if you avoid dealing with a problem again and again, the situations surrounding it become more and more painful each time the condition is repeated.

There is much debate over whether or not we really can remember our past lives—whether, in fact, we reincarnate at all. Do our experiences during past-life recall sessions represent actual, historical lifetimes? Or symbolic, mythical dramas conjured up by our inner selves to give us a better look at ourselves? In my opinion, it doesn't matter. I believe *all* such information is valid and relevant.

The urge to learn, to gain wisdom, has propelled us into this life and will propel us into others in the future. Deep within us, everything we experience holds potential for our growth and development. As we move on, we move with greater personal power, confidence and wisdom, more capable of expressing our individual talents and uniqueness. Each time we gain a speck of wisdom, a speck of ignorance dies. This is the greatest and most exciting adventure of all.

Social and Cultural Programming

Each time a being chooses physical incarnation, it moves into a climate, culture, family situation, etc., in which it must survive. In order to survive, it must become socialized and enculturated. Thus it begins to adopt values and behaviors that society insists are absolutely necessary for acceptance in that culture.

However, society puts itself first and considers the preservation and continuance of society to be more important than any one being. Beings come and go within a culture. Cultural structures are much more powerful than any personality structure one being can create, since they are the creations of many beings in concert, the culmination of many beings' ideas and beliefs. It's very difficult for a single individual to change or have impact on social structures, even though these structures may be impeding the growth process. If any human being is to survive in its culture, it must encounter, accept and deal with that culture's social laws, customs, mores and beliefs—even if they obstruct the process of becoming wise.

At the basis of all social/cultural programs are paradigms. These are the standards, the truths of a society, its social myths that are promoted as certainties. These are superimposed on every being as it comes into physical existence and they form the restrictions and limitations within which a being will have to live as a member of that society. Only when we become wise enough to discern for ourselves between the real and the illusory, to see which outworn ideologies and paradigms are inhibiting our growth, are we able to become all that we can be.

A cultural pattern existing in every society is that of "right" and "wrong." Another is a system of classifying "superior" and "inferior." Another code which is entirely artificial yet essential for the perpetuation of any culture is the classification of its members, the stratification and social positioning of the beings in that culture. These structures are already firmly in place when a being enters a society. Your place on the scale is one of the greatest inhibitors to becoming what you can become in your culture. These artificial and inauthentic cultural patterns can, and frequently do, control our lives. But at some point, every being has the opportunity to choose whether to retain or drop the cultural patterns it has accepted into its personality out of necessity.

Our personal belief systems define the boundaries of our individual realities. What each of us believes to be true *is* true—for us. If we believe something does not exist, it cannot exist for us. We are all limited by our beliefs.

However, too often our belief systems are based not on personal choices and experiences, but on what has been taught to us by others. We have been programmed to adopt another's belief system as our own without questioning the "authorities." So long as we react mechanically, from our cultural programming, we are the puppets of other people. We certainly are not exercising our abilities to choose. Nor are we becoming wiser by choosing *not* to choose. We need to gain confidence in ourselves so that we no longer have to depend on others to direct us—we can decide for ourselves.

We continually create mental concepts in an attempt to understand the world around us. A concept is a theoretical construct consisting of a central point or idea and all the material that has come to be associated with that idea. When individual concepts are passed on to other persons as though they were truths, they become "cultural concepts." Cultural concepts condition our mental and emotional responses, our behavior, our perceptions and the way we relate to others.

Technique for recognizing cultural concepts: We have "inherited" certain concepts from the various authorities who educated us, principally from our parents, teachers, political and religious leaders. These concepts revolve around some very important ideas.

Get out your notebook and head a page with the phrase "This is my concept about..." and choose one of the following words to finish the sentence: nature, God, parenting, love, violence, success, failure, friendship, selfishness, spirit, truth, soul, ego, self, happiness, personality, patriotism, loyalty, leadership, weakness. Or, use words that you consider important. The concept of sin is one of the most influential cultural concepts ever created, so you may want to start with that one.

Now write down everything that you associate with the word you've chosen. When you've written all you can remember or feel about your word, read what you've written and try to recall where those thoughts originated. From whom did these concepts come and under what circumstances? How have these cultural concepts influenced your experiences and perception? How does this concept make you feel about yourself and your world? Can you recognize this concept as the product of human minds and not necessarily true? Can you detect any attempt to control your behavior or manipulate you in this concept? Understanding how these cultural concepts influence you is the first step in altering them to fit your personal belief system.

Role-playing: When we were children, we liked to play "let's pretend," mimicking adults and modeling our behavior after those we loved or respected. We also played certain roles and adopted behaviors that would ensure our survival, satisfy our needs and bring us what we wanted. As children, we knew that we were pretending, but eventually we came to believe that we *were* the roles we'd created. We forgot we made them up for a purpose!

Let's return to the childhood belief that we can become anything and anyone we choose. Let's be actors and actresses with the ability to play any role—and recognize it as exactly that: a role. Let's drop our role-identities, our sense that we are males or females, mothers, fathers, daughters, sons, leaders, followers, successes, failures, responsible citizens or ne'er-do-wells. Now we can begin to model our role-playing on the best examples available and we can drop any roles that are no longer relevent in our lives. We also can learn to play the role most appropriate to the circumstance. For instance, once you leave your job and go home, you needn't take your job-role along with you. Nor will you want to carry your family-role into your friendships. Learn to drop one role as you take on another—don't mix them up.

You can use your notebook to help identify the various roles you play. Use a different page for each role and describe the way you play it on that page. Now think of others who play a similar role and how they play it. Next think of someone you believe plays this role exceptionally well, and jot down some of the things s/he does that you could use to help you play the role better. Model each role you play after the highest ideal you can conceive of it.

Continue through your list, examining each role you are currently playing. Which ones give you the most satisfaction? Are you getting as much satisfaction as possible from these roles? How do you react to the roles that life has "forced" upon you? Can you accept your culture's attitudes toward your roles or do you need to develop your own style? Are you strong enough to resist others who identify you as your role? For instance, I am a human being who will play the role of "female" throughout this physical lifetime, but I am no longer affected by cultural beliefs about females. I now can create my own ideal of what femininity is and play the role the way I choose.

You are to be congratulated for surviving the deluge of cultural programming which has denied you access to your potential. Here you are, strong enough and intelligent enough to flourish without it. You are now ready to take action to relieve yourself of the burden, suffering and pain such cultural programming inflicts on those who choose to keep it.

Technique for dissolving negative programming: You can use your pendulum to discover your negative programming. It can be particularly helpful in identifying beliefs that begin with "I can't" such as "I can't get well" or "I can't help myself" or "I can't do that." Once you've identified them, you can rid yourself of these hindrances by visualizing them written on a piece of paper. Picture yourself burning or tearing up the paper. If you wish, you can use real paper and actually tear it up. Symbolically, you have disposed of this negative programming and your inner self will get the picture.

Cleansing

During our lifetimes, we have accumulated many beliefs, programs, concepts and attitudes. They cling to us like barnacles on the bottom of a boat. Before we can begin to reprogram ourselves with new directions and ideas, it usually is necessary to clear away some of the old ones.

One way you can do this is by writing in your journal regularly. When you move something that was inside you out onto paper, into your journal, you make space for something new to move in. Often we are so full of ideas and emotions that there just isn't room for anything else. Also, when you express something from your inner world, you help it come into being in the outer world as well.

Emptying the tank: Use your favorite relaxation method to enter a meditative or alpha state. Then imagine you have a tank—like a large water tank—into which you've been pouring all sorts of ideas and emotions for years. The tank is full, and you can no longer use it. Its walls are so thick you can't see what's inside. Now notice that there is a faucet near the bottom of the tank. If you put a bucket under the faucet and open the tap, you can empty some of the contents from the tank into the bucket. Look at what you've poured into the bucket. Now you can see if this represents material you want to save or throw out. If you decide to save it, put it back in the top of the tank. If you find that it's no longer useful to you, throw it away and empty more of the tank's contents into the bucket. Continue this process until you've gotten rid of all your old, worn-out attitudes, emotions and beliefs.

Reprogramming Yourself

Programming occurs on different levels—physical, mental and spiritual—and exists in different realities. When you undertake a new program, it is happening "now" on a mental level. However, its manifestation in the physical realm will take place some time in the future. But you know that this program already exists and has existed from the moment of your birth as the perfect spiritual seed form.

Autosuggestion technique: Begin by composing a series of mental relaxing exercises to prepare your inner self to receive the messages of autosuggestion. Sit in a comfortable chair or lie down. Let your awareness be passive and give your imagination free rein. Now follow the next four simple steps.

1. Close your eyes and reflect for a few seconds on an experience in which you were very relaxed, such as lying in a quiet place in the warm sun or falling asleep after a brisk walk. Recall as much of the experience as you can.

2. Think of a color you like. If it is a bright one, change it to a more passive, relaxing color such as your favorite shade of blue or green. Imagine that color, really "see" it on the backs of your eyelids.

3. After a few seconds, take three deep, slow breaths. Hold the third breath and mentally repeat the name of the color three times.

4. Exhale and go limp. Don't move a muscle. Stay still, calm, relaxed and mentally count backward from 50 to 0 very slowly. When you reach 0, count forward from one to three. Now, open your eyes.

After doing these exercises several times, you may find you lose track of numbers or skip a few. That's okay.

During the first two weeks, practice these exercises three times daily, preferably at different times of the day. Beginning with the third week, cut back to twice daily.

As you increase your general relaxation, you create a context within which autosuggestion can be successful. Now, you can program your inner self to accomplish whatever you want. You can suggest that it eliminate pain, change your eating habits or increase your self-confidence. Repeat each suggestion at least three times or as many as twenty times. When you repeat the suggestion, move your lips as if you were speaking aloud. This helps to reinforce your suggestion to your inner self.

Self-hypnosis technique: This also is called auto-hypnosis. When using this technique, you are reprogramming your inner self to manifest your intentions. You are the designer of your future; your conscious or human self makes the decisions, your inner self carries them out.

Sit in a comfortable chair, close your eyes and use your breathing technique or other relaxation method. Once into an altered state, focus your attention on your inner self which resides in the solar plexus, about two inches below your navel. Focus on your navel if you like. Flood that area with love and appreciation. As you feel your inner self respond to this, begin to silently repeat a keyword, phrase or mantra. It should be a nonsensical word, one without meaning, such as "glotz" or "hist" or "pentrala." When the physical body is in a relaxed, anxiety-free state your inner self is very receptive to instructions, commands and directions. You then can program it with your intentions—whether they are to eliminate unwanted attitudes and behaviors, or to incorporate new ones into your life.

If you haven't had much experience in meditation or communing with your inner self, you may want to use what are called "induction tapes" to help you move into this hypnotized state. Record the following or create your own message, inserting your special mantra or keyword in the appropriate places. Repeated use of this tape will train the inner self in the process of moving from its usual, waking consciousness to a self-hypnotized trance. The object of an induction tape is to shorten the relaxation process so that eventually the trance state will result simply from the sound of the keyword alone.

When you are ready to listen to the tape recording you've made, find a quiet, comfortable place to sit. Wear loose clothing, close your eyes and listen passively to the sound of your own voice.

Induction tape #1: "I am now comfortable and ready to move into a state of calm, clear consciousness, a state of physical relaxation and regeneration. I now accomplish a state of being which is perfect for me to use in self-training and self-communication.

"I now see myself in a dimly-lit elevator. In front of me is a door and above that door is a dial. The dial has the numerals one to ten on it. A pointer rests at ten. The number ten represents the state I am in at the beginning of this process. The pointer moves as I descend into a deeper state of awareness (keyword). As I look at the dial, the pointer moves toward the number nine and I relax more and more. My awareness becomes keener as I become even more relaxed. The pointer continues a steady descent toward eight and my consciousness deepens. It reaches eight and continues toward seven, then past seven to six. I become more relaxed, more balanced, more tranquil (keyword). The pointer continues its downward motion as my mind becomes more clear and aware.

"I am calm and peaceful but alert. The pointer reaches five and moves on (keyword). Moving steadily, the pointer reaches four and continues to three. I am totally comfortable and at ease (keyword). It passes three and goes on to two. When the pointer reaches one it comes to a stop in stillness and complete calm (keyword). I am happy, calm and serene. This state is perfect for communion with any and all parts of my being. In this state my parts move toward a more unified whole. In this state I can call for and receive memories that will aid me in bettering my life (keyword).

"Each time I use this induction, the process will move more swiftly and effectively. Each time I use this process my inner self will become better trained and more skillful in attaining the state I desire (keyword). The word (keyword) will symbolize the serene state accomplished by this process and in the future when I use the word (keyword) my inner self will automatically shift into this state. Each time I move into this state, by way of induction or by hearing the word (keyword) my self will remain in touch with my environment. If any event occurs that needs my attention I will be aware of it immediately and respond to it. I will be able to use this state to dissolve stress and operate from a more perfect awareness. In this state I can think clearly and rationally without reacting to past memories. In this state I can observe past memories thoroughly without being involved with them.

"This state is one of physical relaxation and mental clarity. My inner self is attentive and receptive to programming. It is a state in which my inner self is responsive to my desires, will and intention. Here my inner self becomes quiet and relaxed, secure in my love and protection. To leave this state, all I have to do is desire it and it is accomplished."

You may revise this, lengthen or shorten it or use it as the basis of your own original induction if you like. At the end of the induction tape proceed with whatever programming you have intended. You can tape record an affirmation, intention or goal. As you become expert, you can use your keyword as the door to this state of consciousness and play only the affirmations you have pre-recorded.

The first induction helps you go to a deeper state of consciousness and is useful when there are memories to be explored. The following induction tape uses the symbolism of rising into a higher dimension. This is an especially effective technique for communicating with your high self.

Induction tape #2: "I am now comfortable and ready to move my awareness to a higher state of consciousness. My awareness expands and my scope of perception widens. In this state, communication is prompt, memories are recalled quickly and all thought is clear and concise. In this state, my inner self presents to my imagination whatever I wish. The word (keyword) is the symbol of the state I achieve through this induction—a relaxed, calm, clear and serene state of mind with an equally relaxed and comfortable physical body. As I move into this state, my body regenerates and balances all its functions.

"The word (keyword) brings into existence a receptive state of mind in which my inner self is responsive to all I desire. It accepts all programming I provide. The word (keyword) means perfect harmony between all parts of my being. The word (keyword) is also the symbol for a higher state of mind where super faculties function. I now shift into higher states of consciousness.

"In my imagination I see before me a mountain. I am some distance from this mountain but have a good view of it. My goal is to reach the top of this mountain. I am now moving smoothly and quietly toward the mountain, coming nearer and nearer to it. I see many other people climbing upwards, also trying to reach the top of the mountain. I know that the top of the mountain is a higher state of consciousness where we can achieve unity with many. All who desire this unity—within themselves and with all others—are free to move toward the pinnacle of this mountain. I eagerly look forward to reaching the top of the mountain.

"I move faster as the mountain appears to come closer and closer. Just as I reach the mountain, I feel myself rise effortlessly. I can smell fresh mountain air and I see a path upward to the top of the mountain. I touch down on the path and feel the vitality of the trees that line it as I walk along. I breathe in the freshness of their vitality as I come to rest at the top of the mountain. Here I can see in all directions. Here I have an expansive view from which I can see my own personal affairs. I now have the viewpoint of my higher self and so can see everything in a broader context. Here I have access to wisdom and truth. Here I can set my long-range goals and instill in my inner self the ambition and confidence necessary to meet them. Here my self will accept and work with any program I give it. At any time I desire I can leave this place immediately and resume normal awareness.

"In the future, all I have to do to return to this mountaintop is to say (keyword) and my inner self will achieve it. Immediately I will be in a higher state of consciousness—one that includes physical relaxation and rejuvenation, emotional serenity and mental calm. Each time I move into this state my health will be improved on all levels and my vitality increased. My emotional well-being will be renewed, too. My mind will be keen and receptive to inspiration and wisdom. My willingness to abandon ignorance and accept knowledge will be increased. This is the state where I work on the process of self-actualization and self-fulfillment."

Re-Programming the Physical Body

As discussed in the previous chapter, what we believe about health, illness, our bodies and physical processes will be our "truth." Our bodies reflect what we believe about them. So if we believe, for instance, that we are going to catch colds, that belief will surely manifest as many colds! Similarly, if we believe we are ugly and unattractive, that is exactly the way we will appear to others. In contrast, if we believe we are beautiful and attractive to others, that beauty will manifest regardless of physical features.

It is important to identify the belief systems you hold about yourself physically. Examine your feelings and ideas about your own body. Identify any derogatory ideas and feelings you have so that these can be dissolved to make room for a new program. Some negative programming might not be immediately apparent. For example, I once was told by a doctor that it would take about six weeks to recover from a sprained ankle. Although many people might accept this as true, I did not; instead I programmed myself to recuperate speedily. My ankle was mended in three days!

One erroneous and dangerous belief is that disease and illness attack from "out there," that we are the helpless victims of germs and viruses. We need to recognize the tremendous power within ourselves to deal with any threat to our health. During a flu epidemic, for instance, observe people who don't succumb rather than those who do and try to define what it is that keeps them healthy. Perhaps it is a belief in their own bodies and their power to destroy invading viruses.

As a child, I was amazed by the family who lived next door. The parents were continually exhorting their two children to wear rubbers, sweaters and hats or they'd "catch a cold." The children were so obedient they often became sick with colds! In contrast, the four children in my own family were seldom ill though we rarely took precautions against "catching colds." Since we rarely even thought about colds, we hadn't programmed ourselves to accept them. If, like many people, you believe you "catch colds easily," you may want to change your program to "I used to catch cold easily but I have changed and have developed a powerful resistance to all cold germs."

Visualization technique: To re-program more positive beliefs about your physical body, you want to give your inner self a strong, vibrant vision of it. Envision your body as beautiful, strong, vibrant and healthy. Feel love for all its parts. Admire and honor it. Think about the fantastic miracle of its processes and how remarkably it functions. Marvel at its growth from infancy to adulthood, fulfilling the spiritual design for its flowering that existed from the moment of your birth. That perfect image of you that existed in totality in the spiritual realm is your goal.

The imagery you use to re-program yourself is very powerful and will be interpreted literally so choose the symbolism carefully. See the result you desire and picture it clearly. Empower your vision with the force of your will. Focus your attention on your inner self, confident that it will fulfill your vision. While imagining your goals, be sensitive to any feelings of discomfort or resistance within. If you experience any, explore them further and attempt to resolve them.

Re-programming the Emotional Body

Laughter is the best medicine for emotional illnesses and for many physical ones as well. Children seem to be most in touch with this expression of emotional well-being. They often laugh out of sheer joy, not because anything is particularly funny. Unfortunately, this jubilance is frowned upon by many adults. My sister and I used to laugh uproariously over nothing while washing and drying the dishes—until our parents separated us! Have you lost your sense of humor? Do you still laugh because you are glad to be alive? Like many people, you may be due for a dose of laughter. A healthy laugh should rise from deep within, but many of us have been programmed to titter rather than really laugh. The following laughing meditation can help heal your emotional body which in turn will enhance your physical body's health.

Laughing meditation: Begin your day by laughing for five minutes. This sounds simple, but it usually isn't. Start by saying aloud, "Ha Ha Ha Ha" and keep repeating it as you mimic true laughter. This exercise sounds ridiculous; within a couple of minutes you may see it as absurd and really begin to laugh in earnest. As you laugh, you may trigger healing laughter in anyone else who hears you. Why is this so effective? Laughter lightens the body by dissolving burdens, cares and woes. Seriousness is a heavy, burdensome state and weighs us down.

Often we believe that those who have attained high levels of spirituality are solemn and serious. Actually, the opposite is true. A spiritual person is lighthearted, not ponderous. He or she is able to perceive humor in everything and recognizes the power of humor as a healing agent. The ability to laugh at oneself is an achievement of the spiritually enlightened. Humor is not frivolity—it reveals wisdom, truth and beauty.

Overcoming fear: Fear also interferes with the health of the emotional body. Many of us have been programmed to be fearful and our fears negate our personal powers for creating emotional and physical health. Unfortunately, that which we fear often comes upon us, within the realm of possibility or probability. Some people believe fear is healthy, since it keeps us from endangering ourselves. Although fear does restrict behavior, it is usually to our detriment.

Fears are emotional programs. Since our lives are the result of our mental and emotional creations, our fears are interpreted by the inner self as goals to be achieved. Sometimes the intensity of a fear will increase until it becomes so painful we seek relief by materializing the very things we fear. Then we can say, "I told you so." Fearing for others is not a sign of caring. Rather, it shows that we have no confidence in their abilities to care for themselves or our abilities to cope with their downfalls. A truly spiritual person does not fear for others.

The following affirmations can help you overcome your fears. Use the ones that are appropriate for you, or create your own. Repeat them several times a day. Write them down and place them in a position of prominence—on your refrigerator, above your desk, on your bathroom mirror—where you'll see them frequently.

*I no longer fear what others think of me.

*I no longer fear criticism.

*I no longer fear loss of control.

*I no longer fear limitation, but use it to my benefit.

*I no longer fear the law, for laws exist to help me.

*I no longer fear natural catastrophes, for my inner senses will warn and protect me.

*I no longer fear death, for it is the door of transition to more life.

*I no longer fear being dependent, for I know others care for me.

*I cast out fear of all kinds, for others and myself alike.

*Fear does not help me survive but destroys the quality of my life.

*Fear is not necessary to me or anyone else.

Fear has its own specific emotional pattern that radiates outward as it influences bodily processes. You've probably heard that animals can smell fear. This is indeed true, for the body produces a substance that has a distinct odor and which is emitted in our perspiration when we are frightened. Anxiety is a form of fear. The only solution to overcoming fear is to get rid of its source.

When I was a child, I was terrified of dogs and went to school daily in fear of meeting one. My fear actualized itself and attracted dogs who attacked me—which further reinforced my fear. My parents wisely ended this cycle by bringing a little puppy home. As I grew to love and enjoy him, I overcame my fear. I was never attacked again.

Later in life, I owned a Doberman and his responses to others intrigued me. Invariably, when someone who feared or disliked dogs was present, my dog would lie across my feet and growl softly. If that person came closer to me, he growled louder. He wasn't much of a watch dog, however, as he enthusiastically embraced anyone who loved dogs!

Handling anger: A friend told me once of the tremendous surge of anger she felt upon seeing her hysterical daughter returned from a visit with the child's father. My friend did not express her anger and even experienced guilt about becoming angry. When we talked about it, she suddenly realized her continual suppression of anger was causing her debilitating headaches. Finally she realized that her response was appropriate—of course she had a reason to get angry at the person who caused her daughter's distress. Once she expressed her anger to the child's father, her headaches disappeared.

Some of us need to learn to feel and express anger in appropriate situations. When you perceive an injustice, or cruel or harmful behavior against yourself or others, feeling angry is the appropriate response. Next, it is necessary to decide whether expressing your anger will be helpful in any way. To respond to anger with anger is inappropriate and wasteful; it depletes your energy, clouds your perceptual faculties and perpetuates an environment of hostility.

Not only is it wrong to inflict harm, it also is wrong to allow anyone else to inflict harm on you. One of your responsibilities toward your inner self is to defend it and keep it safe from harm. If you feel anger in response to another's treatment of you, let that other person know that he or she offends you. Sometimes all that's necessary is to point out another's bad behavior and to make him or her aware of it. Take a firm but calm stand and state that you will not tolerate future abuses meekly.

Reprogramming the Astral Body

The astral body is a subtle force field which surrounds every living thing and reflects the emotional, mental and feeling conditions of that being. Although this body is imperceptible to ordinary vision, those who have what is called *aural sight* see it as being full of color. It changes with our thoughts, feelings, emotions, etc., and sensitive people can diagnose health or illness in the mental, emotional and physical force fields by the colors in the astral body.

Color programming technique: You can use color to reprogram your astral body. Use your favorite breathing technique to reach an alpha state of relaxation. Then begin visualizing pleasant, clear, radiant colors that are appropriate for the condition you desire. (See chapters 4 and 7 for information about color.) Inhale the color(s) you've chosen and imagine your astral body replacing harmful and unpleasant emotions such as fear, guilt or resentment with more desirable ones.

The peace program: When the astral body is balanced, you experience a feeling of peace. This exercise can help you achieve this feeling of harmony. It is best to do this meditation lying down and to relax your physical body with deep, slow, rhythmic breathing. Visualize all the colors in the rainbow and begin to draw a clear, beautiful pink into your astral body through the soles of your feet. Imagine pink light filling your form as it moves up through your legs and into your torso. Picture it flowing into your entire body until you are filled with pink light. Visualize that pink subtle body pulsing as you breathe, in and out, expanding and contracting.

Next, imagine golden yellow flowing into your astral body through the top of your head. The yellow and pink light do not merge; both are visible. The pink and yellow lights interact, becoming luminescent and glowing as they touch. Marvel at the illusion of a glowing peach color created by this interaction. It appears to be one color but is actually a combination of yellow and pink and you can distinguish the individual hues. Lie quietly for a few moments, seeing and feeling the pulsing, glowing peach subtle body. Gradually, release the picture and just lie still, feeling peaceful within and at peace with the world.

Reprogramming the Spiritual Body

Programming on this level involves developing a belief in your own spirituality. Through recognizing that this higher condition exists, you activiate your higher perceptual abilities.

As we've already discussed, there is a corresponding higher sense for each physical sense. In the spiritual body exist organs of perception that are dormant in most people. Although these organs often function in childhood, they "shut down" as the child matures due to restrictions and unhealthy cultural programming. All of us have higher organs of sight, smell, taste, hearing and touch which we can awaken and expand, allowing us to experience wonderful dimensions of existence heretofore unknown. The exercises given in chapter 5 and in my earlier book, *Develop Your Psychic Skills*, can help you re-program your spiritual body.

Anchors

An anchor is an object that you associate with a specific state of being. A rabbit's foot is a well-known anchor, but you can use a stone, a crystal, a button or any other small object. Many people use worry stones or rosary beads as anchors. You can make your own or purchase anchors that appeal to you.

External anchors act as directives to your subconscious mind. If stress is one of your problems, for example, you would use an anchor to symbolize relaxation. Whenever you begin to feel stressful, tense or anxious, take out your anchor and hold it in your hand. It will trigger a feeling of relaxation. If you feel you need more patience, choose an anchor that symbolizes patience for you. You may wish to have several anchors, each one representing a different condition you want to achieve.

After you have selected your anchor, you'll want to imbue it with the quality it is intended to inspire. Sit quietly, breathe slowly and relax. Hold your anchor in your hand. Close your eyes and repeat the name of the quality—patience, courage, confidence, serenity—three times. As you say the word, sense your inner self's response to it. Next, recall a memory of a time when you felt this quality strongly. Remember that this state of being is always available to you, for it comes from within you. Now bring to mind someone you know who embodies this quality. Think about that person and share the desired quality with him or her for a moment. Focusing on the object in your hand, again repeat three times the quality that will be triggered by this anchor.

Carry your anchor with you and reach for it whenever you need it. You can call your anchor a trigger, if you prefer, or a token or totem. You also may wish to create anchors to arouse feelings that have gone dormant in your life—amusement, tolerance, compassion, acceptance, joy, pleasure, spontaneity, love, caring and forgiveness are a few possibilities.

Finding Purpose and Meaning in Life

The purpose most of us pursue is the satisfaction of needs. Needs may be divided into three basic categories: physical, social and higher (or meta-needs). Once our physical needs for food, water, shelter, etc., have been fulfilled, we are free to move toward satisfying our social needs, for companionship, love, the approval of those we respect. When these needs have been met, we can begin to fulfill our meta-needs, which include self-fulfillment.

The inner self does a remarkable job of achieving goals, but it does not initiate them. This is the role of the aware, human self. Before your inner self can satisfy your needs, your human self must provide clearly-defined goals as well as the direction, motivation and guidelines for achieving them. Have you ever wondered why at times you felt lazy, uninspired, depressed or apathetic? At those times, your human self was not doing its job, not providing direction for your inner self. Your human self must give your inner self a reason to get up in the morning!

So long as we find purpose and meaning in our lives, we continue to grow, to expand, to enjoy living. Our subtle bodies radiate warmth. We experience pleasure and satisfaction. But sometimes the goals we've accomplished come to the end of their usefulness and no longer have meaning for us. When we cling to old goals and behaviors which have outlived their purposes because we fear the unknown, we stop growing. Our physical and subtle bodies begin to lose their warmth and the process of decay begins.

Some entities cling to their etheric bodies even after physical death. Their etheric shells act as shrouds or covers which block their perception of everything beyond the earth plane. An earth-bound entity such as this experiences its etheric body growing colder and colder. This is the reason a cold presence is usually associated with ghosts. People who spend their physical lifetimes clinging to outmoded behaviors, attitudes and conditions, who never learn to release fears, guilts, resentments and regrets, are more likely to become ghosts than those who readily change and move on.

When accomplished goals no longer have meaning for us, they must be shed to make room for new goals. For example, when I was a child, my goal was to grow taller. Of course, when I became an adult, it was no longer necessary to hold on to that goal.

Eliminating Outworn Behavior

Quite often, old, outworn, useless behaviors and attitudes keep us from moving forward and accomplishing new goals. Your inner self is a creature of habit and clings to old purposes and intentions until you command it to eliminate them. So long as a program is in your inner computer, it will keep printing out—until you erase it from your memory bank! This tendency is rather like carrying on outdated traditions that have lost their meaning. A family I know always trims the ends of a roast before cooking it. This method of preparation has been passed down from mother to daughter for generations. When one of the daughters in the family asked *why* the ends were cut off, only a great-grandmother could remember. It seems that *her* mother trimmed the ends of the roast because her only roasting pan was too short!

Identifying outworn behavior: The first step toward ridding yourself of old, useless habit patterns is to identify them. Use your notebook again and make a list of some behaviors, attitudes, beliefs and habits that no longer serve a purpose in your life and, in fact, may be interfering with new goals and purposes. Your list might look something like this:

*Making others feel guilty
*Becoming ill to get sympathy
*Avoiding something or someone
*Asking for trouble to relieve boredom
*Punishing yourself to relieve guilt
*Seeking retribution for a hurt
*Seeking validation of a poor self-image
*Trying to change or "save" others

Erasing outworn behavior: Your inner self is image-oriented. Therefore, it responds best to pictures and visual demonstrations. Here are some ways you can demonstrate graphically your intentions to eliminate old behaviors and attitudes and set your inner self to work cleaning house.

Take the first statement on your list of outworn behaviors and write it on a blackboard with chalk. Look at it for a moment, then erase it. As you wipe the slate clean, affirm that you now eliminate this program from your life because it no longer has meaning for you. Continue down your list until you have erased them all.

If you prefer, you can write each useless behavior in turn on a scrap of paper, then burn it. Affirm your intention to eliminate it from your life as the paper burns. Burying the scraps of paper in the ground is another effective method of showing your inner self that these behaviors are dead and gone. Or, you could flush them down the toilet.

If you feel you need a little time to gradually release the old behavior, carve the message in a bar of soap. Then affirm that when the soap is used up, the behavior will have disappeared. Any other technique you feel will get your intentions across to your inner self is okay; these methods are only suggestions.

Separating Needs from Wants

Advertising focuses on our wants not our needs. Its goal is to weaken the will while strengthening desire. To retain power, our government ignores our real needs, promoting desires and demoting will. Too often, our parents confused our needs with their needs. As a result, it's not surprising most of us have some trouble distinguishing between our needs and wants.

One way to begin differentiating between the two is to use your notebook again. Write NEEDS at the top of a page, then divide the page into two columns. In one column, list "needs" you can fulfill yourself using your own will; in the other, list "needs" that require someone else to satisfy them. Which list is longer?

Now look at the column which involves the participation of others. Try to recall how and where each need originated—did you initiate it or did someone else? What would happen if the other person(s) refused to cooperate in satisfying your needs? How would you respond? Could you manage independently? Could you get by without having those needs fulfilled? Do these needs make you dependent on another, or benefit someone else at your expense? If so, these may be wants instead of needs.

Every plan or goal we set for ourselves is related either to our needs or our desires. Therefore, it is important to determine our current positions and orientations before we can focus on future purposes and goals.

Sometimes we may feel we lack the power to get what we want and need, but usually this is not true. Remember, we create our own realities. Consequently, what we more frequently lack is the will to get what we want and need.

Pendulum exercise: You can use your pendulum to discover how strong or weak your will is. Draw a horizontal line and write STRONG at one end, WEAK at the other. Now holding your pendulum between your thumb and index finger, let it swing of its own accord to indicate the condition of your will at this time.

You can use the same sort of line to determine how strong or weak your desires are. Often desires limit will. For example, if you strongly desire approval and praise from others, you are sure to limit the expression of your own free will.

Setting New Goals

Anything you want intensely enough can be yours. We all have heard stories of people accomplishing incredible feats when their desires and purposes were strong enough, such as saving the lives of loved ones by lifting cars to free them. We never really know what we can do until we believe we can do it and try. Christ expressed this when He told followers they could move mountains if only they had faith the size of a mustard seed.

As you begin setting new goals, ask yourself what purpose will be accomplished when the goal is reached. If your goal is to make more money, for instance, ask yourself what will be achieved by making more money— what is the purpose behind the goal? Will this allow you to pay your bills or enjoy some of life's luxuries? Will it enable you to send your kids to college? Will it give you a chance to travel and see the world? Will it bring you attention and status in the eyes of others? Be sure, too, that you evaluate the potential of harming or helping others in the process of accomplishing your goals.

Remember that behind each physical incarnation we assume is the greatest purpose of all: to gain wisdom and lose ignorance.

Technique for reaching your goals: On a piece of paper, draw a series of circles starting at the far left hand side and reaching to the far right hand side. The first circle on the left side represents the beginning, the last one on the right side represents the goal.

Now recall some time in the past when you had a clearly-defined goal and write that goal in the last circle. Think back to the time when you knew your purpose but had not yet realized it. Write this in the first circle.

In the circles between the two extremes, list the steps you took to accomplish your goal. Above and below those intermediate circles, list the side issues, deviations, events, influences, etc., that transpired or related to this process of reaching your goal. Take your time and make this chart as complete as your memory will allow.

When you've completed your chart, go down the lists and put a star beside each step or side issue that helped you progress toward your goal. Now consider a current goal you wish to achieve. Can you use any of the steps you've starred on your chart to help you reach your new goal?

Years ago, I read an article in a women's magazine which posed the question, "If you could give your children only one gift, what would it be?" Included in the article were the responses of some famous women, and as I read their answers—happiness, success, wealth—I thought, "Something's missing." I thought a long time about what my gift to my children would be and finally the answer came to me. If I could give them curiosity they wouldn't need anything else. They'd find all those other things themselves. Their curiosity would lead them to success, friendship, fulfillment and all sorts of wonderful things.

Curiosity never dies. We are born with it, and though many of us bury it beneath our daily cares, responsibilities and activities, it is always there, waiting to be sparked to life again. Lots of us experience a resurrection of curiosity during what is called the "midlife crisis." The luckiest of us never lose it.

Reading this book shows that you are curious, and—having gotten this far—determined. Because you are curious, your pursuit will lead you to your answers.

Notes

1. Lawrence J. Bendit and Phoebe D. Bendit, *The Etheric Body of Man* (Wheaton, Ill.: Quest Books/The Theosophical Publishing House, 1977), p. 14.
2. Enid Hoffman, *Develop Your Psychic Skills* (Gloucester, Mass.: Para Research, Inc., 1981), pp.130-138.

Enid Hoffman

Enid Hoffman is a well-known author, lecturer, teacher, counselor and lifelong student of parapsychology, metaphysics and transpersonal psychology. She is also the author of three other books: *Develop Your Psychic Skills, Huna: A Beginner's Guide* and *Hands: A Complete Guide to Palmistry*.